# WILD TURKEYS
AND
# TALLOW CANDLES

Growing Up in Granville
Before the Civil War

First published in 1920 by The Four Seas Company.

This edition published in 2004 by the Granville Historical Society.

Afterword © 2004 Granville Historical Society.

ISBN 0-9755757-5-9

*Additional copies may be obtained from:*
Granville Historical Society
P. O. Box 129
Granville, Ohio  43023-0129
Phone: 740-587-3951
Email: office@granvillehistory.org
Website: www.granvillehistory.org

# WILD TURKEYS
### AND
# TALLOW CANDLES

———

## Growing Up in Granville
## Before the Civil War

ELLEN HAYES

Formerly Professor of Astonomy and
Applied Mathematics in Wellesley College.
Author of *Calculus with Applications*,
*Letters to a College Girl*, etc.

GRANVILLE HISTORICAL SOCIETY
*Granville, Ohio*

TO

## Brice, Stanley, and Winchell
GREAT-GREAT-GRANDSONS

OF

## Silas Winchell and Ruby Rose Winchell
THAT THE FUTURE
MAY BE LINKED WITH THE PAST

# PREFACE

One October day in 1917 a far-traveled Pierce-Arrow car paused on the highway half a mile east of Granville, Ohio, and turning to the left took its course southward down a steep grade into an uninviting by-road. Going a few hundred yards it was stopped by a bridge, obviously frail, and the occupants of the car continued their explorations on foot. Where was that ever-flowing stream of artesian well-water which once came into existence when borings were made to find coal? An old woman from a solitary house explained that a disagreement over boundaries had provoked one of the parties to plug the pipe, and so the water flowed no more. Since when had cows been grazing in the mill-race—once the home of catfish and mud-turtles? Just where did the forebay reach across the cart-road from the race to the big wheel—that leaky forebay with its ever ready shower-bath? How long had the mill itself been gone? The automobile turned back and took its pilgrims to a district north of the highway. "The frost is on the punkin and the fodder's in the shock" where formerly a willow-bordered mill-pond had welcomed skaters and fishermen and swimming boys, according to the season. Was there not corn-land enough in Licking County that Norton Case's good mill-pond should be thus sacrificed? A visit was made to a certain hillside orchard—an orchard once famous for miles around. It seems that apple-trees are not everlasting; though they out-live the hand that plants them, they too pass into old age and disappear.

On all sides, on other streets no less than on this Centerville Street, marked changes—no doubt locally termed "improvements" were in evidence. Very much of Granville's earlier material environ-ment had gone in the making of those improve-ments—gone beyond recall and beyond any picturing except such as words may form. A day or two later, one member of that October pilgrim party, coming along eastward on a twentieth century train, began to see reasonableness in a suggestion to describe the life of the Granville of 1850–1860. It is the illusion of each generation that what is well-known and definite today will always be so. Hence, records are inadequate and incompletely kept; important letters are de-stroyed; precautions against fire are not taken; and of course the duplication of documents is held to be superfluous. In another decade or two there will be hardly any one living who will remember the great Middle West as it was just before the Civil War. This fact is sufficient reason for the im-mediate writing of as many local narratives as pos-sible. Upon such mid-century cross-sections must be based the future studies of that region and epoch. My own recollections cluster around one

Ohio town some twenty-eight miles east of the capital of the State; in recording these recollections my object has not been biographical, certainly not autobiographical. I am only trying to picture the life of those long ago years in that Granville town as a child saw the life.

As regards material for Part I, all who are acquainted with Bushnell's *History of Granville* will recognize my indebtedness to that work; and next to Bushnell's book I am under obligations to Isaac Smucker's various historical writings. Both of these authors rendered signal service to Licking County and so to Ohio itself by their timely collection of historical material. It is perhaps not necessary to mention other writers of Ohio history —a rather long list has been consulted—but from all their books I single out one, now unfortunately out of print: Morris Schaff's *Etna and Kirkersville,* a book as charming as it is unpretentious, written by a man whose experiences in cities and on battlefields seem to have rendered only the more unfading and imperishable the recollections of his pioneer boyhood. I have kept this book at my elbow to remind me constantly that I am not writing history in Part II; I am only developing some negatives personally acquired long ago. General Schaff has the advantage of me by eleven years' seniority; he remembers more things and remembers them in greater detail than I do. Yet it will be seen that I share with him the happy distinction of belonging to the pioneer epoch. We lived in different though neighboring communities; and I can at least hope to supplement his narrative with further sketches of those tallow candle days.

It is, however, to my brother Stanley that I must express my greatest obligation; for this little book owes its existence to him. Without his initial suggestion and later encouragement it would not have been undertaken. "The Society of Descendants of Henry Wolcott," which he has served as president, realizes to what an unusual degree this Granville-born descendant holds it both a duty and a privilege to honor the colonial ancestors. It is just and suitable that this Sketch should be dedicated to the children of Stanley Wolcott Hayes. I take the liberty of doing so, quite without his permission or knowledge.

E.H.

E. Wellesley, Mass.
October, 1919.

# CONTENTS

Introduction .............................. 1

## PART I: WILD TURKEY PERIOD

I.    Early Ohio ............................ 9
II.   A Vanguard of Neighbors .............. 15
III.  The Pioneer Journey .................. 20
IV.   A Land of Promise .................... 26
V.    The Wilderness Home ................. 31
VI.   The Pioneer Motive .................. 46

## PART II. TALLOW CANDLE PERIOD

VII.  Centerville Street .................... 55
VIII. An Octagon of Education ............... 64
IX.   The Wolcott Homestead ............... 72
X.    The Year Around ..................... 82
XI.   The County Fair ..................... 95
XII.  Autumn Days on the Farm .............. 104
XIII. A Child of the Ohio Eighteen-Fifties ....... 114
XIV.  Early Institutions ..................... 137
XV.   The Burnt-Out Candle ................ 151
Appendix ................................. 161
Afterword ................................ 166
Map of Granville & Vicinity (circa 1889) ........ 172
Granville Historical Society .................. 174

# WILD TURKEYS

AND

# TALLOW CANDLES

———

Growing Up in Granville
Before the Civil War

# INTRODUCTION

## THE WORLD'S WANDERERS

*Cras ingens iterabimus aequor.*
—HORACE.

The morning twilight of human history reveals man as a migrant. That primitive creature could hardly have been anything else, considering that he must have inherited from his prehuman ancestors not only the habit of moving from place to place, but also those material conditions which initially induced the habit. Climatic changes, failure in food supply, the lure of better hunting-grounds, better fishing-waters, were no doubt the earliest causes of wide wanderings. Closely related to these causes was the friction between groups or races, more powerful groups dispossessing weaker ones and occupying their lands.

Whatever the minor to-and-fro motions, east and west, north and south, in Eurasia the migrations which were primary both in order of time and of importance were from east to west. Thus the mighty Cro-Magnon race of some 25,000 years ago either drove out or exterminated the Neanderthal men and occupied the region that is now southern France. These hunters and artists built their hearths and chipped their flints quite unmindful

that the grottoes which were homes to them were
to become museums of prehistoric material. But
the skull preserved beside the hearth was Asiatic,
declaring in the fulness of time not only that the
Cro-Magnon had been a migrant, but also that he
had come from a land far to the east.

These paleolithic men of Western Europe were
not the last, even as they had not been the first, to
enter a land that was either one of refuge or conquest. By the land-bridges and the valley ways, by
mountain passes and island stepping-stones, in the
Eurasian part of the globe race has followed race,
checked by nothing but the "wet sea," the
Atlantic, and probably not even by that in a time
so early that a land-crossing could be found by way
of Greenland. The conquest of the Atlantic itself
was reserved for a later day and a modern world.

Man's migratory activities fall, broadly speaking, into two classes: the moving bands go either as
plunderers or pioneers. In the former case the
action, on whatever scale conducted, is essentially
a raid and is made with intention of return; that is,
it is reversible. The operations of Attila and of
Jenghiz Khan were of this type. On the other
hand, migration proper, or colonizing, is distinctly
non-reversible. The home-hunting journeyings of
the Hindus as they may have poured through the
passes of the Hindu Kush into the valley of the
Indus furnished a fair example of permanent colonization. In true pioneer enterprises men have
always taken their women and little ones with
them, they have taken their house-gear, their folk-
ways and folk-lore, and the places of advance in

human culture have been determined by these colonizing movements.

The adventure which consisted in the trans-Atlantic migration though a very recent one must be regarded as coordinate with the east-to-west land migrations which began at least three hundred centuries ago. Other thousands of years will no doubt need to slip away before history can adequately portray the effects of that Atlantic leap, shared in as it has been by most of the races to whom modern Europe has been home. We may know history in the making, but the scroll which is as yet so completely rolled only allows us to guess that the fates of races and the nature of new civilizations are bound up with the spread of Europe over America.

The story of the early West Atlantic seaboard colonies is too familiar to require rehearsal here even if there were space and purpose for telling it. The object of this book is to deal in narrative fashion with a single thread of that transcontinental weaving of colonization which proceeded from the Atlantic to the Pacific in the latter part of the eighteenth and first part of the nineteenth centuries. This particular thread of the continental fabric was tied in 1805 to a certain point in Central Ohio to be known from that year as Granville.

The reverse side of migration is invasion. The Indians of the Mississippi Valley and beyond were called upon, first of all, to face an invasion represented by individual explorers, hunters, trappers, and traders. Through the report of this unorganized advance-guard the white settlers east of the Alleghenies learned something of the regions beyond. It was inevitable that daring companies should set out for the great West with other purposes than those that governed the hunter and trader. The day of the colonist followed that of the vagrant adventurer. To secure, however, the proper political and social background of even one colony it is necessary to sketch briefly the outlines of the early history of the Middle West.

France's claim to North America, due to Cartier's discovery of the St. Lawrence in 1534, naturally conflicted with the claim made by England which was based on Cabot's discoveries in 1497. Cartier's discoveries were strongly supported by those of the intrepid LaSalle made more than a hundred years later (1670) when he reached the Ohio River. In 1682 LaSalle floated down the "Messipi." His explorations of the Ohio and the Mississippi may deservedly be called the discovery of the great Middle West although De Soto had reached the Mississippi before him. The French government always based its claims to the Ohio Valley on the exploration made by LaSalle. Thus the official instructions sent to M. du Quesne in 1752 recited:

> The River Ohio, otherwise called the Beautiful River, and its tributaries belong indisputably to France by virtue of its discovery by Sieur de la Salle; of the trading posts the French have had there since; and of possession, which is so much the more unquestionable as it constitutes the most frequent communication from Canada to Louisiana.

The struggle between France and England for ownership ended in 1763 when France formally ceded to England her possessions lying east of the Mississippi. Great Britain held these possessions only twenty years, that is, until the close of the Revolutionary War, 1783, when by the Paris Treaty of peace, British America was limited to the region north of the Great Lakes. Virginia, rather than the United States, technically acquired the Northwest through its several charters granted by James I, with dates ranging from 1606 to 1611. In 1783 the General Assembly of Virginia passed an Act authorizing the Virginia delegates in Congress to convey to the United States all the right of that Commonwealth to the territory northwestward of the river Ohio. March 1, 1784, Thomas Jefferson and three others, Virginia's delegates in Congress, did, as per deed of cession, "convey in the name of and for, and on behalf of, the said Commonwealth transfer, assign and make over unto the United States in Congress assembled, for the benefit of said States, Virginia inclusive, all right, title, and claim, as well of soil as of jurisdiction to the territory of said State lying and being to the northwest of the river Ohio."

After such language as this, one may feel reasonably sure that the said territory is well and truly conveyed; though any holder of a deed to real estate in that region, considering the origin of his title, may be tempted to ask how James came by the land.

It is impossible that France or England or the United States could have realized in the eighteenth century either how vast or how valuable was that territory northwest of the river Ohio. The New World was too new to Europeans for the full significance of its possession to be clear to them. Even in the second decade of the twentieth century, having been overrun rather than occupied, its possibilities are unrecognized by the majority of its inhabitants. The practical end of some forms of its exhaustible natural resources may be alarmingly near, but with a thriftier and more scientific system of agriculture, including reforestation, the old Northwest Territory shall yet afford prosperous homes to additional millions of citizens.

Having thus secured title to this Virginia territory the United States published in July, 1787, "An Ordinance for the government of the Territory of the United States north-west of the river Ohio." This document came to be known as the "Ordinance of '87," and for internal reasons it was also sometimes called the "Ordinance of Freedom." It provided a property qualification for the electorate and assumed that women were automatically politically outlawed through the circumstance of being women.

This Ordinance of Freedom concludes with six "Articles of Compact" between the original States and the people and States in the said Territory "to remain forever unalterable unless by common consent."

Article 1 relates to religious liberty and provides that "no person demeaning himself in a peaceable and orderly manner shall ever be molested on account of his mode of worship or religious sentiments in said territory." From which we may infer that similarly he shall not be molested on account of lack of any mode of worship or absence of religious sentiments.

Article 2 is substantially a bill of rights. "The inhabitants of the said territory shall always be entitled to the benefits of the writ of habeas corpus and of trial by jury, of a proportionate representation of the people in the legislature, and of judicial proceedings according to the course of common law. All persons shall be bailable unless for capital offenses. All fines shall be moderate and no cruel or unusual punishment shall be inflicted. No man shall be deprived of his liberty or property but by the judgment of his peers or the law of the land."

Article 3 provides that "religion, morality and knowledge being necessary to good government and the happiness of mankind, schools and the means of education shall forever be encouraged. The utmost good faith shall always be observed toward the Indians: their lands and property shall never be taken from them without their consent; and in their property, right and liberty, they shall never be invaded or disturbed unless in just and lawful wars authorized by Congress; but laws founded in justice and humanity shall, from time to time, be made for preventing wrongs being done them, and for preserving friendship with them."

Article 6 declares that there shall be neither slavery nor involuntary servitude in the said territory, otherwise than in the punishment of crimes, whereof the party shall have been duly convicted. This article, however, concludes with one sinister proviso under which a fugitive-slave law might have been framed and justified.

On the whole the Ordinance afforded a dependable basis for the constitutions of States that were to be formed out of the great Territory. Barring its stupendous, albeit unintended, injustice to women it was a document of "civilization, and therewith citizenship—the skill to behave in a civilized world," as Professor Myres, author of the Dawn of History, so felicitously defines citizenship.

# PART I

# WILD TURKEY PERIOD

## CHAPTER I

# EARLY OHIO

"They said, the Buckeye leaves expand
Five-fingered as an open hand,
Of love and brotherhood the sign—
Be welcome! What is mine is thine!"

The early history of Ohio would be somewhat simplified if there were any records of the pre-colonial settlers. But hardly more is known of the individual "squatters" than of the ever-roving trappers and hunters. These frontiersmen recognized no law or land-title except what was termed the "tomahawk-right," registered with a tomahawk on a forest tree. They made small clearings, built cabins, raised crops for a few years and then perhaps moved on to some other point. As a rule they antagonized the Indians who shrewdly perceived the nature and consequences of the coming of this white-faced foe. Historical justice—the only kind now possible—will never be done the Indians of the Ohio Valley until it is frankly admitted that the white man was an invader, opening his invasion by doing wanton injury and provoking violence in return. The story of the devoted but ill-fated Moravians affords the chief if not the only record of honor on the part of the coming people in those years preceding 1787. The Moravians must be regarded as forming the first company settlement; they were also the first whites to discover a way of justice and humanity for dealing with the Indians; but they, in common with their Indian friends, fell victims to savage white men.

It should not surprise us that the Indians fought desperately and in their own fashion for the lands of their fathers. It was a defence that would have been honored as nobly patriotic if made by any European people. But in a racial struggle so unequal there could be only one outcome. In their defeat at the battle of Fallen Timbers, 1794, the Indians recognized their fate. The treaty made the following summer was signed by ninety chiefs and delegates from twelve tribes, including the two famous chiefs, Little Turtle of the Miamis and Blue Jacket of the Shawanes; while their conqueror, General Wayne, signed for the white man's government. Perpetual peace and amity were declared; the tribes placed themselves under the protection of the United States, trading territory for sums of money agreed upon and the prescribed "protection."

The settlement of the Indian troubles, added to the formation of the Northwestern Territory, led naturally and promptly to a distinct movement for colonization. Indeed, various companies of colonists were already on Ohio soil prior to the Treaty of 1795. The Ohio Land Company, formed in Massachusetts, purchased a large tract of land in 1787, the same year, it will be observed, that the Ordinance was passed. The actual group of pioneers representing this Ohio Land Company, under the leadership of Rufus Putnam, established a settlement on the banks of the Muskingum in 1788. "I have seen no place that pleases me so well for settlement as Muskingum," reported one of the Company's explorers; and there at the point where the first large northern tributary enters the Ohio they built Marietta the Buckeye State's earliest town. Washington's estimate of the group led by Putnam is probably just and unexaggerated: "they were men to whom education, religion, freedom, private and public faith, which they incorporated in the fundamental compact of Ohio, were the primal necessities of life."

Later in 1788 John Symmes with a company of thirty colonists having for their destination the valley of the Big Miami started from New Jersey, crossed the mountains and struck out for the Miami country, a region that had been described to them as "the fairest meadows that ever can be."

During the next fifteen years settlers either as single families or in groups made their way into the region north of the Ohio, usually coming down the river by boat to the mouths of the northern tributaries and then ascending these streams. Thus settlements were made on the Muskingum, the Scioto, the Big Miami and the Little Miami. These streams were natural thoroughfares and gave access to the interior before anything that could be called a road was yet in existence through the dense forests. These pioneers came from Massachusetts and Connecticut, from New Jersey and Pennsylvania, from Maryland and Virginia and Kentucky. The population of the new Territory was thus composite from the start.

Due to this train of migration the Territory governmentally organized in 1788 was able to show, fourteen years later, a sufficient population between the Ohio River and Lake Erie to justify the formation of a State, and in 1803 Ohio was admitted to the Union. Thirty-five men formed the Constitutional Convention and drafted the Constitution which was adopted by unanimous vote, November 29, 1802. By the enabling Act of Congress this was final and a reference to a popular vote was not required. A proposition to submit the Constitution to the electors was, however, introduced but defeated by a vote of 7 to 27. Thus the Constitution went into effect at once. But even if the members of the Convention had recognized the essentially undemocratic character of their action and had been without authority for such action it would have been most difficult to submit the proposed Constitution to the electorate for ratification or rejection. The people were scattered here and there through the forest with trails rather than roads and little traveling at that; for most of them Chillicothe was a long way off, through the woods, as measured by facilities for letters or messengers. In so far as they concerned themselves with political developments in their wild wide country they knew that their delegates would undoubtedly enact a constitution based on and in harmony with the Ordinance of '87. And, as the sequel showed, Ohio did become the first-fruits of that Ordinance.

One of the immediate expressions in recognition of the advantage of having an actual State to settle in was the formation of the Scioto Land Company in 1804. This company was formed at Granville, Massachusetts, a town in the southeastern part of the Berkshire Hills. As their name indicated they proposed a settlement in the Scioto Valley, but as matters turned out, the tract actually selected was on a small stream which, with others, forms a western tributary of the Muskingum River; they therefore changed their name to the Licking Land Company and under that title their Constitution was adopted.

In the spring of 1805 an exploring and surveying party was sent out by this land company to select and purchase a tract for the proposed colony. These agents selected and bought 29,040 acres in the valley of Raccoon Creek, one of the "forks" of Licking River, the Muskingum tributary above mentioned. By an Act of Congress in 1796 a broad belt of land—more than two and a half million acres running east and west through the centre of the region which was to become the State of Ohio—had been set apart to satisfy certain claims of the officers and soldiers of the Revolutionary War. This tract known as the "United States Military Lands" became available for buyers and settlers, and it was from these lands that the Licking Land Company made their selection.

While yet in Massachusetts the Company provided through their Constitution that in laying out the new village a town plot should be reserved;

also, a school lot of 100 acres for the support of schools in the village; also, a minister's lot of 100 acres for the support of "the gospel ministration within the purchase of the Company." It is further recorded that all mill-seats were to be reserved—a significant instance of pioneer municipal ownership, to which was later added another case: when the town spring was deeded to the town for public use forever. After the report of the surveying and purchasing agents to the Company in Granville preparations for the move were made, and September of that same year, 1805, found the emigrants on the road.

## CHAPTER II

# A VANGUARD OF NEIGHBORS

They blaze the trail, they find the ford,
For camp-fires new a spring beside;
Share corn and meat, their frugal hoard—
True comrades in a wood so wide.

In order to realize that the Granville colonists were not going into an absolutely unbroken wilderness it is important to note chronologically some of the various pioneers who were already located in the upper valley of the Licking and its "Middle Fork," the Raccoon; and who, consequently, would be neighbors of the new-comers.

In the spring of 1798 Elias Hughes, born on the Potomac, and John Ratliff, a nephew of Hughes, with their families moved to a point some twenty miles up the Licking from its mouth. They put up their cabins on the north bank of the river about four miles east of the place where Newark was later built. Theirs was, so far as is known, the first white settlement in the territory which now forms Licking County. The location chosen was a spot which, once discovered, could hardly fail to attract and hold them. Any first frontiersman searching for a cultivable island in the forest sea would be satisfied after reaching "Bowling Green" as the place was presently called. It was a level, untimbered bit of prairie ready for planting—probably an old corn-field which Indians had earlier made. The two white men at once proceeded to raise a crop on their ready acres. During the next ten years or more the Bowling Green must have been a welcome feature that broke the monotony of the journey for all pioneers coming up the Licking trail.

Incidents relating to the arrival of certain colonists who were more directly connected with the settlement of Granville township may be described in Henry Bushnell's words:

> One evening in the late autumn of 1800 a settler from the valley below was threading his way through the forest along Ramp Creek, a tributary of the south fork of Licking River, hunting for deer, when he came unexpectedly on a camp-fire. Around it were gathered five men: Benoni Benjamin and three brothers-in-law—John Jones, Phineas Ford, Frederick Ford—and the fifth a man in Mr. Jones's employ. They were exploring with a view to settlement, having left their families back on the Scioto. John Jones was a Welshman, born in New Jersey, and the visitor was Isaac Stadden who afterwards became the first Justice of the Peace acting within the limits of Licking County. These two men soon recognized each other as old acquaintances, having been school-mates in their boyhood in Northumberland, Pennsylvania.

Having found a locality that pleased him Jones brought on his family early in the spring of 1801, unaccompanied, however, by his friends who had selected places elsewhere. He built his cabin near a spring at the foot of a hill on land which afterwards became the Munson farm. This historic cabin "was about ten rods south of the spring, or halfway to the track of the road as first used. Centerville Street being afterwards laid out straight through the plain now runs thirty or forty rods south of this spot". During the same summer, 1801, Patrick Cunningham, from County Tyrone, Ireland, arrived and built the second cabin in the territory of Granville township to-be—about fifty rods north-east of the Jones cabin and near another spring. He is credited with setting out an orchard and cultivating fruits and vegetables. Bushnell remarks that in 1889 the remains of the cabin and nursery were still to be seen. One wonders how Cunningham was able to set out an orchard. Did he bring apple-seeds which he planted, or was he acquainted with some spot on the banks of the Licking or Muskingum rivers where Johnny Appleseed had done his horticultural missionary work?

The next colonists to appear on the scene were also Welsh. Theophilus Rees and Thomas Philipps, well-to-do citizens of Caermarthenshire, South Wales, had, in 1795, sold out and come to America, bringing with them many of their neighbors to whom they had supplied means for the journey. Brief stops were made in Chester County, Pennsylvania, and then in Cambria County. In 1801, or possibly earlier, Rees and Philipps purchased from a Philadelphia dealer in western lands 2,000 acres in what is now the northeastern quarter of Granville township. Rees and a son-in-law visited their purchase in 1801. Later in the same year Mr. Rees sent his son John to put up a cabin and

clear some land which he was to sow in wheat so
as to furnish bread for the family upon their
arrival the following year. John carried out this
plan, cleared the land, sowed the seed wheat and
harrowed it in by dragging brush over the ground
with his own hands, his horse having strayed away.
He then set out to return to Cambria County on
foot. It is related that "arriving at the Ohio River
near Fort Pitt, now Pittsburgh, much to his surprise and very much to his gratification he found
his horse standing on the bank patiently waiting
for the waters to flow by so as to enable him to
pursue his homeward journey. From that point
man and horse went on together to their
Cambrian home in the Alleghenies."

In 1802 Theophilus Rees himself came out with
his family, accompanied by his sons-in-law, David
Lewis and David Thomas with their families. That
first wheat-planting must have been fairly success-
ful, for it is recorded that David Thomas carried a
bushel of wheat on his back to Zanesville, a
settlement on the Muskingum, and brought back
the flour. Mrs. Rees then baked a wheaten loaf the
first made in the township. "The neighbors'
children were all invited in to help eat it as a
curiosity and luxury." These neighbors were certainly few and the children must have been mostly
grand-children.

About the same time came one Jimmy Johnson,
from the vicinity of Wheeling, who bought land of
Mr. Rees and built a cabin on it. In 1803 the Welsh
settlement was further increased by two more
families and in 1804 two sons-in-law of Jimmy
Johnson arrived. Meanwhile a man named Parker

came from Virginia and built a cabin near the mouth of the stream later known as Clear Run, a point perhaps a mile and a half in a southwesterly direction from John Jones's cabin. Parker cleared four acres of ground and planted a patch of corn and garden vegetables. It is recorded that he hired a man to tend this garden-patch, though one is compelled to wonder where he found the man. At any rate, he went back for his family and brought them through safely to the new home; but he himself lived only three weeks after reaching the spot he had chosen and worked on. The eldest son then took charge of the place and gathered the large crop of squashes which his father had planted. The squashes were piled in a rail pen with corn stacked about it for safety. A band of some fifty Indians were camped near and like kindly neighbors occasionally brought a haunch of venison to exchange for squash, so that Mrs. Parker and her children had sufficient food and some variety. They were not long without white neighbors, however, as another settler soon joined them and built a cabin near their own.

## CHAPTER III

# THE PIONEER JOURNEY

> Adieu, my friends! Come on, my dears,
> This journey we'll forego,
> And settle Licking Creek,
> In yonder Ohio.
> —TIMOTHY SPELMAN.

This was the pioneer situation in the upper Raccoon Valley in 1805 when the colonists representing the Licking Land Company were ready to start from Granville, Massachusetts. The historian of that period commenting on the personnel of the emigrant party was moved to remark:

> We could spare our young ministers and young physicians and even our deacons, [sic] but when the strength and beauty of the church and parish were demanded the loss was irreparable.

And James Cooley, in a Jubilee address at Granville, Massachusetts, in 1845, says of those who went west forty years before:

> A long journey of seven hundred miles was before them. No railroads, no canals or steamboats. A mere overland journey through swamps and untrodden deserts; a constant toil by day and by night for more than forty days. But they were the chosen spirits of New England, legitimate sons of old Granville who shrunk at no hardship and feared no peril.

"Swamps and untrodden deserts." One must regret that as late as 1845 any person could so describe the land through which the colonists were to journey. There were no deserts and the wilderness was such as to promise the blossoming rose. Cooley does not overstate, however, the pluck and hardihood of those Berkshire Hills pilgrims. They were of the same blood and spirit as the New Englanders who, more than a hundred and sixty years before (1643), had broken the "Old Connecticut Path" through the eastern wilderness from Boston to the lower valley of the Connecticut River.

How did they outfit for the journey and for the home in that western country? These men were all of them well-to-do for their day, quite able to pay for their individual lots of land when the time came; but whatever their wealth in home-gear the capacity of their ox-drawn wagons must have been quickly reached, considering the nature of the roads they were to travel. Treasured pieces of furniture, prized books, unnecessary clothes and bedding, extra farm implements—all had to be left behind. There must be room for such tools and bedding as were indispensable, room for the Dutch oven, the iron kettle and the bags of flour and corn-meal. Spinning-wheels no less than axes and flint-lock muskets were on the list to go; knitting-needles and garden-seeds had to be thought of, as well as the bible and hymn-book. And when everything else was in there must still be space for the little children and others who could not walk all day. One gallant young mother, Ruth (Rose) Winchell, made the entire journey on horseback carrying in her arms her baby Rebecca, then less than a year old. Probably other mothers travelled in the same way. All things considered, it is hardly surprising that "the oldest among them were serious and provident and the youngest were moved to song by the romance of the situation." Timothy Spelman seems to have been their song writer and some of his verses—not wholly complimentary to the Berkshire country—were sung at their gatherings through the summer as preparations for departure were made.

Instead of moving as one united company they divided into parties with short intervals of time separating the dates of going. In the month of September families began to leave in small companies for their six-weeks' journey. Their route from Granville, Massachusetts, lay southwestward, crossing the Hudson River at Fishkill Landing or Fort Edward, thence over a point of New Jersey, across the Delaware at Easton, the Schuylkill at Reading, the Susquehanna at Harrisburg, by Carlisle and over the Alleghenies, through Washington, Pennsylvania, across the Ohio at Wheeling, and on to Zanesville. From that settlement on up the valley of the Licking River there could have been hardly more than a trail, indicated by blazes on the trees, which had been made by the few wayfarers who had gone before them. Assuming that their trail was blazed by way of Bowling Green they undoubtedly passed through the small settlement of Newark located in 1802 where two creeks, the North Fork and South Fork, unite to form the Licking River. It seems probable that they forded the Raccoon Creek near its junction with the South Fork, went through

Cherry Valley and crossed the Raccoon again some two miles from the first ford, that is, somewhere west of the point where the creek swung sharply against the hill in the base of which the "Dugway" was later made; and thus they entered the little plain east of the place already selected for the location of their village—practically at their journey's end. By such a route as this they would avoid all the hills on the right, westward from Newark, and a creek to be forded must have been much less of an obstacle than a hill to be climbed.

The first company to arrive consisted of William Gavit, Elias Gilman, Levi Rose, James Thrall, Samuel Thrall, Silas Winchell, and their families. With them was Thomas Sill, a man without his family if he had any. They had been forty-four days on the road; it was Saturday, November 2, when they reached the Jones cabin. Saturday evening? one is led to ask. If so this would explain their stopping; for this premier group "kept the Sabbath through-out the journey stopping early Saturday evening so as to have all the preparations made and begin holy time at sundown according to their custom." At any rate they evidently halted at the hospitable and elastic Jones cabin and not only spent Sunday there—within two miles of their actual destination—but waited until November 12 when a second and larger party overtook them. The important event of this day, November 12, seems to have been a religious service, a Presbyterian minister from Pennsylvania happening to be on hand to conduct it. "Scarcely waiting to loosen the oxen from their yokes, or to eat, one hundred assembled for public worship."

The next day, November 13, 1805, they all "hitched up" and drove on, not by a straight trail as Centerville Street runs today; the ox-teams of 1805 were not laying out a street, for they must have wound slowly and uncertainly among the great trees and made many detours to get past fallen ones. They forded Clear Run, probably at some point near the reserved mill-seat where the Winchell flouring-mill was later built, and keeping a last noble hill on their left they entered the public square-to-be and made their final camp.

What were Ruth Rose's thoughts as she handed down the baby and slid from her horse for the last time? Was the exhilarating sense of rare adventure subdued by the certainty of toil and hardship in the life which she faced? It was mid-November and rain threatened. The next meal would have to be prepared as on so many days before, campers' fashion; then she with other mothers must plan to keep the children snug and dry. Did the wild beauty of her surroundings win its way through her senses to a responding heart? The darting fish in the pools, the scolding squirrels, the asters and goldenrods massed in untended glades and defiant of frost, the plump chestnuts and hazel nuts well out of their burs and strewn among the leaves, the friendly stars revealed after nightfall through breaks in the clouds that matched breaks in the forest roof—were all these able to spell their welcome to the tired home-seeker? We shall never know, for she left no common record. It may well be that, whether among the Berkshire Hills or those of central Ohio, Ruth Rose saw more than she mentioned and felt more than she told. There is a chance, more than an eighth of a chance, that traits of hers, passed down, account in a large part for certain traits in one of her descendants: Charles Willard Hayes, (1858–1916), leader of men, lover of nature, geologist.

CHAPTER IV

# A LAND OF PROMISE

The connection between the physical features of a
country and the history and temperament of its
people has hardly received, either from historians
or geologists, the attention it deserves. Though
not obtrusive, it is real and close, and amid other
and more potent influences has never ceased to
play its part in the moulding of national character
and progress.

—ARCHIBALD GEIKIE.

To what sort of a land had the concluding miles
of their journey brought the colonists? It was a
favored country, geographically and geologically
considered, for nowhere else along the entire
southern boundary of the region formally covered
by the continental ice-sheet have the topographic
effects of the great glaciation taken more kindly
and advantageous forms than those that may be
found in Granville township of Licking County,
Ohio. A contour map of this county would show at
a glance that Granville township lies on the limits
of the hill country. Fifteen miles or even ten miles
to the east the contours would indicate steeper
slopes, higher hills, deeper valleys; while to the
west they would exhibit the levels or wide low bil-
lows of land that reach to Columbus and far

beyond. In Granville township there is plenty of rich "bottom" land bounded or broken by hills which are, however, not so steep as to interfere with pasturage needs. Stored away in these hills, conveniently near their tops, is a superior quality of freestone, the fine-grained Waverly—the region, geologically viewed, occupying an intermediate position between the Sub-carboniferous sand-stones further to the east and the Devonian lime-stones on the west.

Somewhere between eastern Massachusetts and central Ohio a brook becomes a "run" and a small river turns into a creek—acquiring incidentally the pronunciation "crick." At the bases of the Granville hills numerous springs, valuable be-cause deep-seated and pure, gave rise to runs which meandered across the lower lands to empty into the creek. The Raccoon, usually a gentle stream and of no great size, was nevertheless a dominant feature of the region on account of its relation to the neighboring topography. This creek had a valley within a valley. Beginning at the bases of the hills there were wide reaches of land, practi-cally level, which dropped by a steep sharply-defined bluff to the bottoms through which the creek ran and which it over-flowed at times of high water—the spring freshets. The historical tense is here used, because it is probable that not a few of the springs have been unable to survive the removal of the forest trees from their mother hills; "the running brook is dry"—or nearly so, and today no one would need to search to find a place where he could cross the creek without swimming his horse.

But to the colonists in 1805 more impressive than hills or streams was the forest. Everywhere, on the tops and sides of the hills, over the creek terraces, over the bottoms to the water's edge, were trees—units in a forest the like of which cannot possibly be seen again while civilization endures between the Ohio River and the Great Lakes. Black walnuts, butternuts, chestnuts, oaks, hickories, maples, elms, beeches, white-woods, lindens, sycamores, poplars, ash, buckeyes, mulberries, cherries, locusts, dogwoods, struggled everywhere for standing-room, for elbow-room and for sunshine. This list is not exhaustive, nor does it give the various species that may be covered by one name as in such cases, for instance, as the oak, the maple and the poplar; but it indicates the marvelous wealth and variety of tree-life in that primeval forest. Shrubs and bushes supplemented the trees, yet not usually in such a way as to make an obstructing undergrowth. The papaws, hazelnuts, sassafras, grape-vines, black haws, elders and spice-bushes watched their chance and knew their place which they clung to with determination. Lowly yet lovelier plants gave the final touch of grace and beauty to this world of growing things.

Furthermore, it was a country that had not been manhandled. Civilization had not entered and begun the strewing of its unsightly *debris*. The moccasined Indian slipping along his indistinct trail had not marked his camping-spots with tin cans and broken bottles, coal-ash heaps, discarded barbed wire and refuse papers. Only one who has searched for a clean spot—a bit of grass fit to rest on—in the suburbs of European cities and towns, or the United States towns, for that matter, can adequately appreciate in imagination the cleanliness of the New West. The land was clean and the streams, large and small, were pure. The sweet limpid waters of Clear Run were good enough for the baby's bath or the tea-kettle. Untainted it took its way over the shining little sand-bars or rested under wholesome clay banks where willow shadows fell until it joined its big brother the creek. Dearly loved Clear Run! Born of springs in the North hills and singing along to the Raccoon, what indignities have been offered you in this hundred years. Who will now believe that you were once well named? The white man's civilization has wronged you into kinship with sewers and factory drains; but you shall at least run through these pages with all the purity that was yours in prehistoric times.

Why did these Granville colonists select for their town a spot so hemmed in? They must have seen that that last high hill which they had passed, along with "Sugar Loaf," its companion hill on the west, would firmly put a stop to east-and-west streets that might wish to continue on a straight and fairly level course; while the range of hills to the north quite forbade convenient growth in that direction. Southward a growing town would promptly drop down to the freshet-swept bottoms. Had the Centerville plain with its ample reaches been chosen the early rivalry between Granville and Newark for place as the official town of the county might have resulted in favor of the former. In that case, Granville could hardly have been the

Granville of this story. We are not left, however, to speculate on the motives of the settlers. One early historian, Jacob Little, says:

> The Company having heard much of the fever and ague as well as the fertility of the West, wished a location which would avoid the evil and secure the good; contain hills for health and level land for fertility. The level borders of the creek through the centre of the township with the rising hills at a little distance on both sides governed the agents in the selection of this place.

In other words the curious group of hills where Granville nestles served to attract rather than to repel. It is also not unlikely that the large spring which the exploring agents must have discovered at the foot of one of the north hills was no small factor in determining the site of the town. This spring was probably much larger than either of the springs near the Jones cabin. An abundance of good water at hand was even more a consideration with the frontiersman in locating his cabin than it is with the modern explorer in pitching his camp for a night or a week.

## CHAPTER V

# THE WILDERNESS HOME

Tell me a tale of the timber-lands—
Of the old-time pioneers;
Somepin' a pore man understands
With his feelin's well as ears.
Tell of the old log house—about
The loft and the puncheon flore—
The old fi-er-place, with its crane swung out,
And the latch-string through the door.
                    —JAMES WHITCOMB RILEY.

Henry Bushnell probably secured for his History of Granville all the facts that will ever be available so far as the history of those first days and the earliest years is concerned. From his records, based on oral or written accounts, we know about the cutting of that first tree, the beech, when the men properly enough took turns at swinging the axe as if it were some communal ceremony. That shelter for four families, made by putting poles across from the fallen tree to stake supports with brush and blankets to form the roof, must have been the model of temporary shelter for all the others. It rained for the first three nights, the roofs leaked and the brush-piles on which their beds were spread rested in water. But they had arrived. No more yoking of the patient oxen to go forward on a trail. All effort now could be spent in making themselves comfortable for the approaching winter. In the midst of their camp labors the Sabbath came—there were no Sundays in early Granville, only Sabbaths. This first day of rest was a memorable one for people who had organized their colonial church the preceding May and had enjoyed the privilege of having a special sermon preached for them before setting out on their journey. Any public service would need to be in the open air, but there was the stump of the beech-tree ready for use as the essential part of a pulpit. An hour was appointed and the horn gave the signal for the gathering of a congregation that numbered ninety-three. Two sermons were read by Mr. Rathbone, one of which was, most appropriately, the sermon that Dr. Cooley had preached more than six months before at the organization of their church. The prayers were offered by Timothy Rose, Lemuel Rose and Samuel Thrall. It is a family tradition that Silas Winchell's wife was a sweet singer and that she led the singing that day. At any rate, they sang and the story is that the sound of the music rose to the hilltops where Theophilus Rees was hunting for a lost cow or two. The far-off lowing of the colonists' oxen led him in their direction until he heard the singing. Looking cautiously over the brow of the hill he saw strangers gathered for a meeting. Without making himself known he hurried home to tell his wife that "they had some new neighbors, of whom she need not be afraid, for they had got the ark of God among them." If this story is not true it is good enough to be true; and one hesitates to point out the improbability that so large a company of settlers could arrive at the

Jones cabin, stay ten days, be reënforced by a larger company, and then move on a couple of miles to their destination without Deacon Rees's knowing all about his new neighbors—even though he spoke no English.

By December 10, 1805, the members of the Company were ready for the division of their land. At public auction bids were made for choices. The land was valued to every member of the Company at $167.30 per hundred acres, each one paying, in addition to this, for his choice of location whatever he bid. Each one hundred acres drew a town lot and for the choice of these, bids were again received. The total amount of "choice" money was subsequently divided among the members according to the quantity of land each one purchased. Some paid nearly as much for their choice as they did for their land, while others paid nothing for a choice. The first farm lot, bid off by Timothy Spelman, was the one adjoining the town on the northeast—plainly desirable not merely on account of its nearness to town but chiefly because Clear Run watered it. The largest purchase as regarded acres was that of Jesse Munson who received a deed for 1500 acres at the Company's price. With his bids added, his tract cost him $3,043.80. This Jesse Munson was advanced in years and only came to be with his children. It is told that when the colonists crossed the Ohio at Wheeling he was disappointed in the soil and looks of the new country and muttered, "If they hadn't anything better than that to show him he should give them a big gun and go back again." But when they reached the Licking Valley his feelings changed; he would get out and examine the soil with his hands, even smelling and tasting it, expressing the greatest satisfaction. Upon reaching the Jones cabin he decided that there would be the place for him to anchor, and he said "he would have that farm." Being a man of determination as well as means he got it and on it he spent the remainder of his life. Jesse Munson also secured the town lot containing the great spring; with admirable public spirit he gave a lien to the Company providing that the spring should be for community use "as long as water runs." It may be added here that Elias Gilman coming a little later into possession of this spring lot confirmed Jesse Munson's intention of public ownership by giving a deed in which he renounced all title to the spring and as much ground around it as might be needed for water-works, if the inhabitants should thereafter see fit to use the spring for public good.

There seems to have been no dissatisfaction with the working of their land-division scheme. By trades and private sales each member was satisfied. In a letter dated January 15, 1806, Timothy Rose wrote: We have come to the division of our land, and that peaceably; and, as I believe, honestly.

With community needs in mind early action was taken to get a school-house ready for the winter. No other community action indicates more distinctly what stuff these colonists were made of; for certainly most groups under like circumstances would have said: "Next year, next spring; we can do nothing for the present except to keep ourselves warm and supplied with food." But in very early Granville education was a business that would not admit of postponement. Samuel Thrall, Lemuel Rose and Elias Gilman were made a committee; as a result of their planning a large log house was built on the south side of the public square. "This was a magnificent building," says one who attended the school which was taught the latter half of the winter by Mr. Rathbone; "the windows were of oiled paper, the seats were shaved puncheons laid on blocks, and the desks were of the same, fixed to the logs of the house at a suitable height by pins set in auger-holes." The building was also used for religious meetings and town gatherings; so it must have been the heart of the settlement in those first months. The first teacher—and reader of sermons—was probably Thomas Rathbone who came with the company which arrived November 12.

Another primary and urgent need, though a more material one, was water-power mills both for sawing logs and grinding grain. In anticipation of this the Company had sent out a small party—five men with their families—in the hope that one or more mills might be in operation on the arrival of the colony. Bushnell writes:

They were Timothy Spelman, Cornelius Slocum, John Phelps, Ethan Bancroft and Hugh Kelley. Mr. Bancroft found shelter for his family in one of the cabins at the mouth of Clear Run. Mr. Phelps and Mr. Spelman in the Jones and Cunningham cabins, and the others here and there. Mr. Spelman seems to have had an oversight of all the workmen, and charge of all the Company's work; and in his absence this care devolved on Mr. Slocum. Mr. Phelps was the millwright and Mr. Kelley the blacksmith. They put up a sawmill about sixty rods below the mouth of Clear Run, on the left bank of Raccoon. The creek made a bend to the south and back again to its original course, and across the neck of the bow was a natural sluice-way which they used for a feed-race. They made a dam at the entrance of this cut-across by setting sycamore logs on end, inclining down stream, and secured a fall of a few feet. But the freshets were too much for the anchorage of the sycamore logs, and the bed of the stream was soon washed clear of them. . . . Afterward, the mill was removed to the head of the cut-across, which was made the tail-race; and, as the first dam had proved a failure, they tried one made of brush. This lived to see the saw run part way through the first log when a freshet came and it, too, was swept away.

There was no sawmill when the colonists arrived—only a story of western freshets—though the millwright had evidently done his best. By some peculiar reasoning they seem to have concluded that Nature or Providence in the form of high waters would be more indulgent to a scheme of private ownership. They therefore offered at public sale their mill-seat at the mouth of Clear Run "together with the mill, the machinery and all the appurtenances." It is recorded, however, that following this sale "the citizens turned out for the public good and helped James Thrall, into whose possession the mill-seat had come, to put in a third dam, made of logs and heavily covered with gravel which succeeded better than the others." It is noteworthy that they so easily lost faith in a community enterprise which, under individual ownership, required the public shoulder at the wheel to make it go.

Samuel Everitt, Jr., returning to Massachusetts for his family, added to the equipment of the Thrall mill by bringing out a new saw blade. The first lumber sawed with it was therefore given to Mr. Everitt who used it in building a house some two miles west of town on lower Loudon Street. He consequently had the distinction of living in the first frame house or, more properly, plank house built in the township. The planks were placed upright and dovetailed into the sills and plates; the cracks were battened and later the structure was weather-boarded with wide boards. Such a pioneer house did no doubt deserve the honor of the rose-bush which was brought from Massachusetts and planted by the east window.

This same Samuel Everitt, besides bringing his family and the saw blade and the rose-bush, brought also the town library which he had been commissioned to purchase. We are told that these books, "being of a high order, were a source of improvement to their many readers for succeeding years."

The Everitt plank house could not long have remained the only one of its kind; for besides the Thrall sawmill one was built by Augustine Munson in 1806 on the creek about two and a half miles east of town. The Munson mill could turn out 4000 feet of lumber per day.

As for grist-mills the colonists' main reliance in the very first years was a mill in Newark. It was women's work not merely to bake the loaves of corn-meal, but first to go miles on horseback to a mill with a bushel or two of grain to be ground. This, that the men need not leave their heavier work. In an adjoining township (Union) Phineas

Ford—one of the men who sat around that Ramp Creek camp-fire in 1800—built a grist-mill on Ramp Creek, making millstones out of glacial boulders found in the fields. There is apparently no record that the Granville people resorted to this mill, though it would be strange if they did not do so; for it must have been quite as near as Newark and, also, Ford had an orchard of fruit-trees grown from seeds which he had brought with him from New England; some of the first apple-trees planted in Granville were taken from the Ramp Creek nursery. Thus the neighbors on the north were not unacquainted with the Ford place, nor was the road thither an untraveled one.

In their struggles with the creek, the most obvious source of water-power, the possibilities of Clear Run were apparently overlooked for a time, but about 1811 Daniel Baker established on the little stream a shop for the manufacture of wooden dishes. Plates, porringers, bowls and spoons were here made, the dishes being turned upon a lathe run by water. Again, about 1816, a flouring-mill was started by Grove Case and Silas Winchell. This mill stood a few hundred feet from the point where the Newark road crossed the run. A head of water was secured by damming the stream a short distance northwest of the mill and forming a considerable pond there. Later a carding-mill was added to the grist-mill. And at least once more Clear Run was put under bonds for a supply of energy. A dam below the grist-mill with a long head-race winding around the foot of the opposite hill gave water to a sawmill built in what must have been the neighborhood of the Parker cabin. This particular sawmill stood near Raccoon Creek, but was wholly dependent on Clear Run for its power.

Distilleries were early erected and there seems to have been no public or private disapproval of the drinking habit until about 1830 when temperance reform began to be agitated. Indeed, whiskey was regarded as one of the necessaries of life, taking rank with meal and meat. In the first winter four leading men of the settlement made a toilsome journey through the woods to Chillicothe, a distance of sixty miles. They went with their oxteams and were four days in traveling the first twenty-six miles when they reached Lancaster. The round trip required three weeks; but they secured flour and with it what they no doubt prized as much—a supply of whiskey.

While there were apparently some whiskeyless days and flourless days the colonists knew no meatless ones. The woods in which these new homes were built abounded in game. Bushnell writes:

> Wild turkeys were so plentiful as to become a pest to crops. They went in flocks to the size of a hundred, and some of the settlers say five hundred. When they began to sow, there are instances of where the sower set down his wheat to club back the turkeys. In the Autumn, the Burg Street hills echoed with their noise, and sometimes seemed almost covered with them. The people did not pretend to eat all they killed. The breasts were torn out for 'jerks,' that is, to smoke and dry, and the rest was thrown away. Those who could not bear to see the waste forbade their young people firing on them. So late as 1811, six years after the settlement, Enoch Graves paid Spencer Wright nine fat turkeys, caught in a pen, for three pounds of sole

leather. A turkey that had been shot came flying
overhead and fluttered down by the side of Mrs.
Winchell, while at work out of doors. It was unable
to fly further, and so furnished them a dinner.
When dressed it weighed twenty-two pounds. A
peddler from Chillicothe stopped at Owen
Granger's tavern one Monday noon, where he saw
several fine turkeys. He bargained with Leveret
Butler for one hundred such, to be delivered at Mr.
Granger's the next Saturday noon. Butler went
home, run his bullets, went out in the afternoon
and in two hours killed twenty-nine. A rain came
up and wet the guns, and he was obliged to stop.
He hung up the turkeys after the Indian fashion,
sticking the head of one through a slit in the neck
of another, and balancing them across a limb. Next
day it rained. Wednesday he went again with one
Nichols, and camped out the rest of the week.
They carried in one hundred and thirty. The wild
cats spoiled six for them. Selecting one hundred of
the best, he delivered them to Mr. Granger and
received his pay. Mrs. Samuel Everitt caught
twenty-three turkeys at one time, trapping them
in a corn crib, luring them to the spot by sprin-
kling a few kernels of corn around. Deacon David
Thomas killed seven with two shots, having a shot
gun and getting the turkeys in a row as they sat on
the fence. Old Mr. Hoover had the name of killing
the largest in the colony. When dressed it weighed
thirty-eight pounds. Mr. Ethan Bancroft shot several that weighed thirty-six pounds.

These turkey stories are worth passing on as an
evidence of the great abundance of this noblest of
game-birds in early Ohio. But there were too many
shot-guns, too many ever-enlarging bare spots
where a strange new enemy strewed grain but carried a club. The turkey was of the wilderness and

in a few decades he was gone from a *habitat* that was no longer his unmolested home.

Besides the turkeys there were deer, wild hogs, opossums, and an occasional bear, so that the meat diet was not without variety. The wolf stories and rattlesnake records clearly show that the backwoodsman's life was more or less beset with dangers, whether on the road or in the woods or around his cabin. To exterminate the rattlers and fight the wolves was merely an item in the program for conquering the country. An illustrative incident occurred in the life of Alfred Avery, the boy who had now found a land where there was "dirt enough to cover the corn." Alfred, having reached the mature age of eleven, was sent one day on horse-back, to the mill at Newark. Returning belated, some animal rushed past him in the darkness and startled his horse, throwing boy and grist to the ground. With the aid of a fallen tree Alfred succeeded in readjusting his load, and so reached home in safety. The animal was believed to be a wolf which happily was not hungry enough to make an attack on horse or boy at that time. Whatever the animal was, the incident has value as indicating that the grist-mill at Newark was early patronized by the Granville folk—even children taking the risk of the six-mile ride through the woods to get the necessary meal ground.

How did life proceed with these colonists, self-planted in a tremendous forest, with next to no exports or imports, with stump-dotted trails instead of roads, thrown on their own resources and equipped with only a slender stock of tools and materials? It is plain that, to begin with, their main dependence must be agriculture, and that meant the clearing of patches in the forest. The fires of destruction were kept going night and day, the year around, just to get rid of timber which a century later would be sorely needed. The magnificent forest yielded to this treatment and in a few years there were spots at least where annual crops could be grown. One common way to get rid of the trees was to make a "deadening." All the trees in a tract were girdled and left standing. As the trees thus treated soon died, root and branch, the ground was no longer shaded by annual foliage, and corn and other crops could be raised among the dead standing timber. This practice of making deadenings was kept up for at least fifty years. As late as 1860 there were large tracts of these dead trees west of Granville. It was a weird and pathetic sight—so many great trees stretching their gaunt and lifeless limbs to the sky as if in protest against the waste and desolation.

The first houses built were naturally of logs with few rooms—one large room serving, like the Roman *atrium,* as the place for carrying on many household operations. The women prepared a break-of-day breakfast in this room while the men were out to feed the stock and give the fires a start. The main breakfast dish seems to have been fresh "johnnycake." As Bushnell tells it:

> The corn meal was stirred up with water and a little white ashes of elm wood or corn-cobs, instead of soda, or a pseudo pearlash made by firing a hollow elm log, the heat becoming so great as to melt down the ashes in cakes. The johnnycake was then spread thin upon a short shaved puncheon.

This was set on end before the fire until one side was baked brown, then turned and baked on the other. Sometimes the rain (coming down the wide chimney?) would spoil one cake, but another would be started at once. When done it was dipped in cold water and immediately rolled up in a cloth to steam awhile, and when it came out "it was the sweetest bread ever made." Potatoes were roasted in the ashes. The breast of turkeys was cut into slices and broiled on the end of a stick or lying on glowing coals. When there was no fresh meat at hand, there was plenty of jerked venison or turkey.

Johnny-cake, baked potatoes and turkey. No mean breakfast for hard-working people, though coffee, butter and fruit are not mentioned. For the noonday meal the breakfast bill of fare was repeated, and presumably supper varied but little, if any, from the two preceding meals. When a real baking-day arrived the women generally used a Dutch oven; that is, a shallow, wide-spreading bake-kettle with a close-fitting cover. This oven was set over a bed of coals and then covered with a layer of coals. Some people used more ample clay ovens that could accommodate eight or ten loaves of bread at a time.

Besides using the Indian corn in the form of meal ground at some mill, this corn was prepared as hominy. A mortar was made by burning in some convenient stump a hollow large enough to hold a gallon or two; a bent sapling and a heavy pestle fixed so as to play over the stump, with a rope and stirrup for footwork, completed the hominy machine.

Bread and meat accounted for, luxuries were found in maple sugar, nuts, dried wild grapes and wild cherries, and, in their season, blackberries,

mulberries and elderberries—together with cran-
berries which friendly Indians brought in for sale.
Finally, when the young apple-trees began to bear,
the pioneer's table called for nobody's pity.

Even as dinner was like breakfast, the work of
the afternoon was a continuation of the work of
the forenoon. According to the season, the men
plowed the ground, or cultivated their crops, or
harvested them, on the ever-enlarging clearings;
chopping intermittently and burning the felled
trees continuously. The women cooked and
cleaned, but their main work between meals was
spinning wool and flax, weaving the spun yarn into
cloth and finally making the cloth into garments
and bedding. The girls were spinsters at sixteen
and spinsters still after they were married. Their
best ginghams—Sabbath-day ginghams—were
made by using hetcheled flax; the coarser tow was
for every-day wear. Shirts and trousers and skirts
must have been easier to come by than leather
shoes; for the habit of going barefooted—at least
in warm weather—was general for both old and
young. People started to church carrying their
shoes and stockings which they put on when they
reached the edge of the village. "But the most daring of the men sometimes came barefoot and in
their shirt-sleeves."

The lack of the simplest of modern essentials—
window-glass, friction matches, baking-powder,
tinware, cotton cloth, tooth-brushes, rubber
overshoes—called forth ingenuity rather than
complaints. These frontier people were without
anaesthetics in childbirth and without antiseptics
for daily hurts. Listerine, carbolated vaseline,

extract of witch-hazel—the commonest articles on the family medicine-shelf today—were wholly unknown to them. But mother-wit, the oldest of all forms of wit, stood by. Pioneers knew the healing roots and leaves of the woods; they knew the therapeutic value of mutton tallow and hot water.

The men toiled unremittingly and were old while yet young in years; but when one considers the work of the women, the conditions under which their work was done, and remembers that the care of babies and little children was a part of that work, it is safe to say that the women carried the heavy end of the load of frontier life. They were, of course, without cooking stoves, or indeed stoves of any sort; and that meant much stooping to cook on the coals of the fireplace with the face and especially the eyes subjected to an injurious heat. From this excess of heat they went to bedrooms that were bitterly cold if it were winter. It goes without saying that their cabins were wholly lacking in bathing and other sanitary appointments. But in health or out of it, having some "things to do with" and lacking many others, these women made the best of their wilderness conditions and devotedly saw their job through to its end, leaving it to their children's children to beat the record of thrift and devotion if they could. Unconsciously and incidentally they furnished reënforcing data for Dr. Dudley Sargent's assertion that "notwithstanding cold, or thirst, or hunger, or physical privation of any sort, a woman can outlast a man."

## CHAPTER VI

# THE PIONEER MOTIVE

And now I have a sheep and a cow, everybody bids
me good morrow.
—POOR RICHARD.

Men to whom education, religion, freedom, private
and public faith were the primal necessities of life.
—WASHINGTON.

Reviewing the circumstances of the first years
one is impelled to ask: Why did these people of the
Berkshires do it? Why did they leave their comfortable dwellings, their white-painted tall-spired
church, and come so far to all this privation and
toil? They certainly had no social or political dissatisfaction with their Massachusetts home. What was
probably the chief purpose of the migration is
revealed in an incident in the New England life of
one of the future colonists, Alfred Avery. "When he
was a mere child his father went out to plant corn,
and himself, anxious to help, took his hoe and went
out also, tugging and sweating to do what a little
boy could. At length his father noticed that Alfred
was crying and asked him what was the matter. The
child's reply was a turning-point in the history of
the family. 'I can't get dirt enough to cover the
corn.' Then the father thought it was time to go
where the world had more dirt. Soon afterward he
became a member of the Licking Land Company."

These colonists were one with the Cro-Magnons and the rest of the long line of migrating peoples in responding to the lure of land further on where they hoped to improve their condition and that of their children as regarded the primary needs of life: food, clothing, and shelter. Each one intended to acquire "a sheep and a cow"—and the esteem accorded to the possessor of fertile acres. In selecting homes in a western State the first consideration was one of average rainfall, average temperature, probable average yields per acre. These matters of their material life being to their satisfaction it was their intention to reproduce such institutions and social customs as they had left behind. No Greek colonists ever guarded more carefully and devotedly the coals taken from the home altars than did these New England colonists cherish the species of religion and government in which they had been bred. So far from chafing under the thrall of precedent or the grip of convention they only desired to render more stable, more distinctly static, the beliefs and habits inherited from their fathers. They were in no sense radicals; they were hardly even liberals, and they habitually accorded scant hospitality to any form of radicalism that appeared among them. A marked example of their natural lack of sympathy with new and unpopular reforms was furnished in the mobbing of the members of the Ohio State Anti-Slavery Convention who came to Granville to hold their anniversary in 1836. We are assured however by one historian that an immediate reaction followed this outbreak and the citizens were filled with shame that such violence should be done in their midst. On the very evening of the day when the mob broke loose, an abolitionist meeting was held in the stone school-house in the Welsh Hills and it was unmolested. "In fact, the abolition party received great accessions as the result of that day's work, and soon Granville became a well-known station on the Underground Railroad."

It should also be pointed out to their credit that a temperance society was formed in their midst as early as 1828; the first one, it is believed, west of the Alleghenies. And from that time on, intemperance there found determined enemies even as the hunted slave, after 1836, found friends. The Granville people, with all their conservatism, thus showed themselves in a measure capable of camping with the vanguard of social progress.

The church, even though early broken up into four or five sects, was their dearest institution. The pastor, as the official representative of the church, was the great man whose teaching directed the thinking and ruled the conduct of his flock. Doctrinal theology laid a heavy hand on them. This earthly life meant to them an experience of providences—of duty and toil, of punishments and rewards, to be followed finally by other-world recompense to those who had "kept the faith."

Yet it must be recognized that their loyal submissiveness to the church and its authorized leaders gave a certain coherence and stability to their standards of right conduct as well as right belief, and served for decades to keep the little community unspotted from an encroaching world.

Next to the church their most cherished institution was the school; for, it hardly need be said, the Granville pioneers were in hearty accord with the uncompromising position taken by the Ordinance of '87, and later by the first Constitution of the State, that since knowledge is one of the three elements "necessary to good government and the happiness of mankind, schools and the means of education shall forever be encouraged." Students of Ohio's early history will recall the scandals connected with her school-lands, the struggles to secure a system of common schools, to recover and properly sell the lands originally designed to support such a system. It is to the enduring honor of early Granville that her citizens went ahead with arrangements for the establishment and maintenance of schools; they could not afford to wait until 1824 when a legislature was finally elected that was willing to address itself to the duty of developing a free public-school system. There were undoubtedly not a few other places that acted thus independently of the State; but Granville waited neither for example nor fellowship in the matter. The spirit in which that log school-house was built in the winter of 1805–6 governed the community for years and led not only to the establishment of the public school but to various private institutions for education.

The "free electors" of Granville had an instinct for politics—politics in the better sense of the word. Elections, office-holding, the machinery of administration, possessed for these frontiersmen an attraction that was perhaps a natural reaction to an opportunity for the creation of a community government. They were young men in a young village and came to their municipal duties unhampered by any past administration either good or bad. The state Constitution allowed a degree of county and town autonomy that was promptly exercised. Thus we learn from official records that

"at an Election Legally warned and held at the School hous in Granville on the 6th day of April in the year AD 1807 for the purpos of chosing townships offisers the Number required in Law having asembled the hous proceded to chose a Chairman and too judges of the Election

Silas Winchell chosen chairman

Isriel Wells
John Edwards $\}$ judges of the Election

Elkanah Lennel
Justin Hillyer $\}$ clerks of the Election

these being quallified according to Law the hous proseded to Ballot for one township Clerk three trustees two overseers of the poor two fenceviewers two apreisers of houses one of with to serve as a Listor four supervisors of highways two constables and one township treasurer"

Seventeen names are given as the officers duly elected "by a clear majority," and the list is followed by the note:

"on Monday April the 13th two of the gentlemen trustees Mess Isriel Wells and Silas Winchell met at the inn hous of Deac Timmothy Rose and took a surity of Joseph Linnel faithfully proformance in the offis of a Constable in the following word and forme viz"

Then follows a record of the note signed and witnessed.

This narrative deals with one township of the county which was erected out of Fairfield County in 1808, but a study of the Licking County settlers as a whole discloses the fact that the Granville colonists from Massachusetts were in many ways matched in nature and character by their nearest neighbors, the Welsh from Caermarthenshire, and the emigrants from Virginia, Maryland and Pennsylvania, who, coming a few years later, settled in a district a few miles southward and gave the names Etna and Kirkersville to their settlement centers. Deacon Theophilus Rees, the patriarch of the little Welsh Hills colony, was quite the peer of the worthiest deacons who came from the Berkshires. We are assured by Isaac Smucker that "Rees was a gentleman and a scholar, a man of intelligence and integrity and great usefulness to his country-men and to the church." Thomas Philipps, lifelong comrade and friend of Theophilus Rees, was also "a well-educated gentleman of large experience and extensive information and reading."

And those Welsh Hills produced one man by the side of whom Granville had none to place. Indeed, the land over, in any time, has few enough like Samuel White (1812–1844) grandson of Thomas Philipps. Smucker, as historian of the Welsh Hills, gives us a character-sketch of White which ought to be passed on and then on. Smucker says:

> White was ambitious in the matter of obtaining an education and entered the Granville College as the first student on the list on the first day of the first term of said college. . . . He was fearless, independent, outspoken, frank, honest, never uttering opinions he did not believe, and always gave

expression to thoughts he entertained, without fear, favor or affection. In the famous crusades of his times against Slavery and Intemperance, he was always in the front ranks, playing the part of Richard the Lion-hearted and playing it well. He asserted the right of free discussion—indeed he became the acknowledged champion of the freedom of the Press and Speech and more than once braved infuriated brutal mobs who tyrannically denied the liberty of speech. Sam White never shrank from the open avowal of his sentiments under any amount of popular odium, and therein he attained in those heroic times to the highest point of independent manhood.

Smucker adds that he and White held opposing political opinions, but were in harmony on the question of the right of free discussion. "I was not in political harmony with him and sometimes not on terms of friendly personal relations; but he had a noble nature and was therefore placable, forgiving, generous, magnanimous." In these words we find evidence of Isaac Smucker's own nobility of character.

In 1844 White received the nomination of the Whig party for Congress in the district composed of Knox, Licking, and Franklin Counties. He died from overwork in that campaign, at the age of thirty-two. And the world had need of him.

It can hardly be questioned that in colonial times Granville had a certain feeling of superiority over other villages and towns of the county. With more hair shirts on its submissive back, more unboiled peas in its pilgrim shoes, than other communities either desired or tolerated, this sense of greater excellence was only natural. The need for neighborliness, the disposition to friendliness induced by wilderness circumstances, must have been all that saved the New England settlement from the charge of phariseeism. But the surrounding settlers left the little hill-encircled town to its zeal for Sabbath-keeping, its emphasis on education, its peculiar notions as to moral conduct, without reproach or envy. This was a time to build, each community in its own way.

# PART II

# TALLOW CANDLE PERIOD

## CHAPTER VII

## CENTERVILLE STREET

No lovelier spot Ohio knows
Than where the restful Raccoon flows,
Where country highways strolling down
In friendship meet at Granville town;

Where stately hills, elate though dumb,
From out the fields of plenty come
And, tree-crowned 'neath celestial blue,
Hold their eternal rendezvous.
—O. C. HOOPER, 1879,
Denison University.

The whole pioneer time in Ohio may be conveniently divided into a Wild Turkey period and a Tallow Candle period. It is not implied that any sharp line divides these two periods; they naturally overlapped. The last of the turkeys were killed probably in the years 1850 to 1855; and they must have been scarce after 1840. The tallow candle began early to compete with the primitive torch and the glowing log-fire for the honor of lighting the backwoods cabin. There were enough candles in Granville in 1840 to enable the citizens to have an illumination in honor of the election of the Whig candidate for the presidency. "Candles in great profusion were prepared, and when darkness came all were lighted up. Almost every window on Broad Street was ablaze, some with a light glowing at every pane of glass." The turkey and the candle serve fairly well to indicate the early and the late colonial times. With the passing of the candle and the coming of the kerosene lamp modern life was fairly introduced. As my own memory runs back to a prekerosene time I am able to describe at first-hand some phases of Granville township life that were essentially pioneer.

The roads radiating from the town were, as a rule, named from the more or less distant towns to which they ran. Thus we had the Lancaster road, the Columbus road, the Worthington road, the Mt. Vernon road and the Newark road. Along these roads substantial and prosperous farm-houses had replaced the original log cabins; although in the period now considered, the sixth decade of the nineteenth century, many cabins could yet be found on by-roads. Most of these farm-houses were two-storied frame structures, with occasionally one of brick, for brickmaking was one of the first industries of the township. The houses were amply supplemented with large barns, sheds, and other buildings required on a well-to-do farm. Vegetable gardens and miscellaneous fruit-trees—apples, pears, quinces, cherries, and plums—flanked the immediate yard and often a regular orchard was to be seen. The modern country-home has backed away from the road, but those first Ohio farm-houses, forgetful of their ample acres, came pathetically out near the road as if looking for companionship. A formal front yard expressed the prevailing fashion in landscape architecture; this yard was more satisfactory if a retaining-wall could be worked in somewhere, while a piece of iron fence established the owner's claim to urban distinction.

If I speak particularly of one of these roads and of one homestead on it, it is not that others were not equally rich in features inviting description; it is only that I knew that road and that home best, and can therefore speak at first-hand. A description of mid-nineteenth century life on one of those Granville farms applies generically to life on the others—allowance being made for such variations as give individuality and character to any home and its owners.

The Newark road, for the first two miles out of Granville, was early named Centerville Street. It had one advantage—or disadvantage—over other thoroughfares in being the road to the county-seat and was consequently more traveled than any of the others. Centerville Street runs slightly north of west and south of east, parallel to the general direction of Raccoon Creek, traversing a level, fertile tract of land which is bounded on the north by the crescent of the Welsh Hills and which extends to the creek on the south. The reach of this crescent is somewhat more than two miles, and from hills to creek the average distance is a little less than one mile. A few gracefully molded, unobtrusive spurs like Alligator Hill extend far enough into the plain to give variety to the Welsh Hills range—on its south side, at least. The plain must have been early cleared for farming both because of its level nature and its rich soil; yet in 1860 many scattered trees as well as wood-lots of varying size remained, while the higher slopes and tops of the hills had hardly been touched by the axeman.

My home was at the western end of Centerville, only a few hundred feet from the left bank of Clear Run; and my earliest associations were with Centerville rather than with the town of Granville itself. Our nearest neighbor, Deacon Wright, lived across the road in a large brick house; his front yard with a high retaining-wall on one side and an iron fence set into dressed stone was, in the eyes of the little children belonging to the small quaint house opposite, a place of such sanctity that there was no danger of its ever being entered voluntarily by them. As if to ward off any approach to the iron fence, hitching posts had been placed some six feet from the fence and connected by rails to which no one ever hitched. Indeed, I was filled with awe if I ever had to pass along the walk, made of brick and bordered with evergreens, which led to the side door. One addition after another gave to the building the effect of trailing away to a distant rear, and it was rendered especially mysterious by having what must have been a basement cellar with an outside door which seemed, like the hitching-posts, to serve no purpose. I know now that the basement of that house was a station on the Underground Railroad. I can remember more than one time when father entered our house and told mother in low tones that "another lot had come."

The poor fugitives were concealed and fed and after dark were carried northward to the next station. But it was not a matter to be explained to little children. I here make honorable mention of that station-master and his wife.

Further down the road on our side—the north side—was another Wright, the "Squire"— "Square" Wright we children had it—living in a stately old home surrounded by maple-trees. Across the way from him was the Wynkoop place where front-yard proprieties were quite set at naught; for the house—a little white cottage— stood far back from the road obviously to make room for the flowers which Mrs. Wynkoop culti- vated with great success. The good lady had a long walk leading from her front door to nowhere; for it stopped among the flowers and was only intended to give the owner access to her beds of blooming plants. How I wanted to see those flowers "near to;" but I never had the courage to go up the drive and ask permission. The Haskell place next to the Wynkoops had one advantage all its own, namely: a lane that afforded us passageway at the side of the fields, down to a bank where a wild cherry-tree grew, past another field and then we were at the edge of the dear old Raccoon. Whether for wading or fishing or merely hunting clam-shells and pol- ished pebbles, that creek drew me as if it were a magnet and I a tiny bit of iron; and the Haskell lane was one of the several easy ways to reach it. On down the road were other farms and other old families; the Aylsworth place, Deacon Rose's place, the Bancrofts, and still further eastward the Robinson farm with its attractive substantial

home built of bricks burnt in one of the near-by
fields; and next to it the Munson farm, the most
famous one in Granville history; for here those
Jones and Cunningham cabins were built near the
springs, and here the two companies of colonists
united for the last bit of their journey. The Munson
farm-house in 1860 was another typical well-to-do
place surrounded by fertile fields which extended
from the hills to the creek. Below it, that is, eastward, were two or three more farms and the limit
of Centerville was reached. The road unwilling to
turn to the south climbed up one hill and down
and then another, and so reached the "Dug-way,"
an excavation made in the side of the hill to avoid
fording the creek. A trip to Newark was regarded
by me as an event and the passage of the Dugway
was the exciting feature of the trip—no matter
what the wonders of Newark might be. For the
road at the Dugway point was a single track without passing-room and it made a sharp curve so
that an approaching team could not be seen until
quite near. On one side, some feet below, was the
creek; on the other, the steep rocky face exposed by
cutting. Supposing we should meet anyone exactly
at the worst place. Supposing! but somehow we
never did. Those Dugway sensations have
returned to me once since in my life: when the *dili-
gence* in which I was a passenger climbed to the
Furka Pass above the Rhone Glacier.

A narrow road bounding the Robinson farm
struck off northward and led into the heart of the
Welsh Hills district. It was a most inviting byway,
woods-bordered, winding about and bringing its
travelers into an unfamiliar region; for the Welsh

Hills country was just beyond walking distance for small feet and we knew only its southern border. Besides this Hills road, two others branched from Centerville but on the southern side; one to Clouse's mill at the head of the Granville "feeder"; the other was the Cherry Valley road which we took when we went to the County fair at the "Old Fort." The mill-road was so near that the dam built across the Raccoon to supply water to the canal feeder was one of our various fishing haunts—esteemed dangerous by our elders, for some grown-up always happened to go along when we made our Saturday afternoon trips.

Of the few spurs that broke the regularity of the Welsh Hills range one, nearly north of Squire Wright's place and about three-eighths of a mile from the road, was known as "Alligator Hill." We could easily see this bluff from our house because no considerable clump of trees or high land shut off the view. My very first notion about the alligator was of a living, crawling beast that might appear any day in our back yard. But as soon as I could walk the distance I was taken across the fields and up the hill to see the wonderful thing. There it sprawled, hummocky and grass-grown and did not move leg or tail. That couldn't hurt anybody. Had I known that some archaeologists would pronounce it an opossum and others declare that it closely resembles a lizard my first conception of the creature might have contained less of the element of fear—assuming that anyone had kindly told me the difference between an alligator and an opossum or an alligator and a lizard. The bluff where this mound is located had been cleared of trees and was in pasture. I never saw it as plowed ground. The "alligator" was a curiosity in the countryside, though probably no one realized the archaeological importance of saving it from plow and harrow. Henry Howe, in his Recollections of Ohio, says that this animal figure is two hundred and five feet in extreme length; greatest breadth of body, twenty feet; length of legs, twenty-five feet; average height, four feet. It is clear, therefore, that with so slight a thickness in comparison with its other dimensions a few years of plowing and harrowing would suffice to obliterate all animal-like outlines.

As the alligator bluff is some one hundred and fifty or sixty feet above the plain and commands an unobstructed view to the southeast of at least eight miles, beacon-lights or other signals could easily have been seen at the mound-builders' works in Cherry Valley if there had ever been occasion to signal to the "Old Fort." The profusion of mounds and other artificial earth-forms in that part of Ohio, and especially in the little Centerville plain and the neighboring Cherry Valley, is convincing evidence that Ohio had once been occupied by a people very different from the Indian tribes which the white race found there. Whence had the Mound-Builder come? When and why did he go? Was it another case of invasion, conquest and migration?

In many lands there are more commandingly beautiful scenes, wilder and grander views; yet one will search far to find any valley that surpassed in winning loveliness that of the Raccoon in 1850–1860 as viewed from one of those southern spurs of the Welsh Hills or, best of all, looking southeast from the top of the hill just east of Granville. The course of the creek was readily traced by the immense sycamores that everywhere fringed its banks; the sycamore had too much individuality to allow its being confused with other trees. The rather low hills and gentle hollows between presented a series of most graceful curved surfaces unmarred by cuts or gradings. Across the creek on the southern horizon the sky met the earth on a range of hills of still less height, wood-covered, tinted in greens and browns and horizon-blues—the pictures in my memory seem to be mostly summer and autumn ones. Often the softest shimmering mist hung over the creek and out of its blue-grey would come the mournful notes of a wild dove. The memory of the cherishing mother Nature that dwelt among those wooded hills and by the running waters is such that I know no other place where I would rather I had been turned loose to live and grow. Through the loveliness of that valley I believed the wide world was lovely, and in its shelter I was prepared to regard the whole earth as home and all the dwellers in the earth as my kinsfolk.

## CHAPTER VIII

# AN OCTAGON OF EDUCATION

To remain ignorant is to remain a slave.
—J. A. WAYLAND.

The heart of Centerville was the school-house situated about midway in the two-mile plain. Built of native freestone, octagonal in form and roofed with a low-spreading octagonal pyramid of shingle-work which was capped with a dressed stone of like shape, this school-house was unique for its day or indeed for any day. It appears from the records of the industries of Granville township that in 1823 one John Jones built a woolen factory "near the stone school-house on the Welsh Hills." There was, then, at an early date at least one other stone building put up for school purposes and belonging to the Welsh settlement. It may be surmised that to Welshmen from Caermarthenshire, with memories of buildings at home, stone seemed the only appropriate material for a school-house, and that they therefore refused to use logs or planks or even brick. The Centerville school-house may well have been built through the Welsh Hills example and influence.

This building stood back from the road and the shade trees of the yard were principally poplars, large ones. One side of the octagon contained the front door, opposite which was the teacher's desk with a small blackboard for background. On the other six sides were desks, high and wide and immovable, with long wooden benches. Seats for the younger scholars were provided just in front of the big desks. These seats were narrow, unpartitioned, and built as part of the desks. Thus the little folks had to sit there without desks of their own, without arm-supports or the least provision for storing away their few belongings. What was worse, the older scholars by reaching over could tweak the ears or pull the hair of the helpless little victims in front. I am obliged to record that advantage was sometimes taken of this situation. I was one of those who sat below in silent dread of the dangers that threatened above. A queer upright stove occupied the centre of the room and bituminous coal was burnt, although wood must have been quite as cheap.

To this school I was sent one happy day when I was just seven years old. As I trotted down the road by the side of the teacher, carrying my dinner in a tiny but gaily-painted wooden pail, my heart beat high with a sense that this was an adventure of moment—as indeed it was. I had learned most of my letters from certain words that stood out in relief on our sitting-room stove, the company name of the makers of that stove; and after that, mother had taught me to read—as an exigency measure: she had no time to read to me. But now I was to go to work systematically, in a school, and I was quite willing to begin at the beginning of the spelling-book with "a-b ab, e-b eb, i-b ib, o-b ob, u-b ub." That school's meagerness of equipment did not impress me then. In my eyes any equipment at all was wonderful. Lumps of natural chalk were used instead of modern crayon. There were no wall-maps and no places for any. The pupils had slates of varying sizes made of real slate set in wooden frames, with gritty pencils, also made of slate. We cherished our few school-books because we owned them, and that ownership often meant a long series of chore-doing. Careful mothers covered the books with cloth—a piece of new calico usually; and this protection was supplemented with paper thumb-covers which we wore when we could remember to do so.

No rare or especially valuable book has ever given me the peculiar happiness that I felt one well-remembered morning when I woke to find a McGuffey's First Reader on the pillow by my head. My father was rather fond of surprises of that sort. It was a tiny, homely book—six inches long and less than four inches wide—and promptly became my most cherished possession, whether at home or on that exposed front seat down at the school-house. Of all the treasures in that treasure-book of literature the one that I prized most was the delectable story of Mr. Post and Mary which begins:

> One cold night, after old Mr. Post had gone to bed,
> he heard a noise at the door. So he got up and went
> out. And what do you think he found? A dog? No;
> A goat? No; he found a little babe on the steps.

This story I read again and again. My fancy never wearied of reveling in the happiness of the old man and the little girl. To me they were real people and might well have lived down the lane near us.

Another book, even more highly valued, was my geography—Smith's Primary Geography, 1855. It also was a small book, in great contrast with modern school-geography text-books. Its pictures —curious old woodcuts of a prephotographic age— took me into far countries, and some of the text even farther away; for from it I learned that

> "The Moon around the Earth doth run;
> The Earth and Moon around the Sun.
> The Earth moves on its centre, too,
> As wheels and tops and pulleys do;
> Water and land make up the whole,
> From east to west, from Pole to Pole."

The formulas of celestial mechanics have never been able to banish or even blur my childish vision of the moon running breathlessly around the earth. This same text-book contained some statements of marked value today in showing how far thought has become freed and knowledge diffused since 1855. Thus in one set of questions and answers in Smith we had:

> Q. When was the world created?
> A. Nearly six thousand years ago.

The author evidently felt it a duty to be more exact, for in a small-type note he adds:

> the creation of the world (reckoning up to
> A. D. 1854) took place 5858 years ago.

Yet such comforting certainties had met their undoing a quarter of a century before in Lyell's Principles of Geology (1830). Lyell was either unknown or his argument rejected by those who were writing our elementary geography books only four years before the publication of the Origin of Species.

My own particular copies of those two books, McGuffey's Eclectic First Reader and Smith's Primary Geography, have long since disappeared with all other things material connected with my Centerville school-days; but it is a satisfaction to know that other copies of them are in the safe-keeping of the Library of Congress.

Our Centerville school was, of course, ungraded; that is, it provided for all grades. But if the freshmen began with "a-b ab" no teacher could be expected to show a senior class of any great advancement. However, in Centerville, the degree of advancement reached in one's studies was unimportant, for within two miles were various other schools where one might study if he were so minded. The great service was to provide an open door out of the bondage of ignorance.

Two gigantic black walnut trees, interrupting the undecided foot-path that straggled past the salients of rail fences, stood by the Centerville wayside in those early days. One was near Mr. Haskell's house; the other, a short distance west of the school-house. Their vast trunks branched into wide-spreading symmetrical tops which shaded the road for many yards around. Their great horizontal reach of limb indicated that they had never suffered from forest crowding. For some reason they must have been spared when the first clearings were made and their fellow-trees laid low. Wagoners rested their horses in these shades and each tree afforded a genuine oasis for children pattering along barefooted through the dust to school. Incidentally their bountiful crop of nuts was a large item in their autumn hospitality. Were these two trees destroyed by storms, or were vandal axes made to hurt them to death with the notion that in their fall and removal the street would be "improved"? They are gone, and the quaint, octagonal school-house is gone, too; though it was well worth preserving as a museum for colonial articles of the neighborhood. In 1860 most of the attics and cellars on Centerville Street probably contained historical treasures that could tell of the pioneer days.

The small pronoun of partnership, *we,* has already been used in this narrative and will be used again to denote a group of little folks hereditarily disposed, even in their tenderest years, to engage in any exploring and primitive living that came to hand. It seems necessary to explain who "we" were. Of the family of children living in the house on the bluff opposite Deacon Wright's place in 1860 I was the eldest and naturally the leader. Next to me was Anna, the unselfish obliging one, ready to take any role in the plays and go to the limit of her energy in our carryings-on. Following her came Orlena, earnest and sympathetic, a genuine pal in devising and executing schemes. I can see her now, her noble Winchell head and sturdy little figure, as she bends to some cooperative task of ours such as damming the tiny run which was trying to make its way through water-cresses and past small engineers to Clear Run. Last of the girls was Mariquita, the "little Mary;" a most winning child, full of daring and needing to be constantly watched lest she crawl under the big gate and start off on expeditions of her own. She was fortunate in being the youngest girl as that placed her next to Willard, who was twenty-two months her junior, and thus they two became special chums. Willard was a silent, gentle child who at first regarded the performances of his sisters with much quiet wonder, but soon entered actively into every plan as if he were as old as any any of us. Besides his silence and gentleness one other characteristic marked him from his very earliest years: he seemed not to know what physical fear is. It might be a drove of steers coming down the road, or just a place in the stream where the water swirled over slippery stones rather too strongly for his little legs—he wasn't afraid; he met the danger, whatever it was, with the same intrepid daring with which, in its frail and hastily-built boat, he ran the Nizina Canyon, Alaska, 1891. Last to join us and one especially welcomed was Stanley, a golden-haired lad, in features and bearing very like Orlena, the sister whom he never saw. But by the time Stanley was old enough to be boosted over a rail fence or to crawl through a board one our father had moved his family to a distant part of the county, and thus the youngest never got his rightful share of the Centerville heritage. The sequel has shown, however, that the spell of his native valley was on him in no less degree than on the rest of us.

Of this group of six two are gone. Orlena was only nine years old when attacked by a swift-working and fatal brain disease—perhaps meningitis. In the twilight of that June day in 1864 when we had looked for the last time on her dear face, the sorrowing parents, sitting by themselves and not knowing that they were accidently overheard, said to each other: "We have lost the choicest one of the bunch." "Yes, we have." I doubt not that they were right. To this hour I grieve for Orlena as for one who has been needed by her family and by the world.

The story of my brother Willard's life has been elsewhere told.[*] It is not necessary, therefore, here to describe how, in due time, he went far afield and brought honor to his native State as a geologist. While yet in the prime of life his strong skilled hands grew frail and lost their hold on hammer and pen, and he, too, vanished into the deep shadows which everywhere border the Long Trail.

"Nothing is here for tears, nothing to wail
Or knock the breast, no weakness, no contempt,
Dispraise, or blame, nothing but well and fair,
And what may quiet us in a death so noble."

In this book Orlena and Willard are two happy little children, keen-eyed and sturdy, roaming together over the fields and through the woods of their pioneer ancestors.

---

[*]Alfred H. Brooks: Bulletin of the Geological Society of America, 1917.

## CHAPTER IX

# THE WOLCOTT HOMESTEAD

Plow deep while sluggards sleep, and
you shall have corn to sell and to keep.
                              —Poor Richard.

An apple a day keeps the doctor away.
                              —*Mother-Lore.*

Sandisfield, Massachusetts, located near Granville
in the Berkshires, had furnished pioneers for Ohio's
first settlement more than half a dozen years before
the Granville colony was organized. Among the
Sandisfield emigrants who went early to Marietta
were two brothers, Horace and Josiah Wolcott,
descendants of Henry Wolcott of Somersetshire,
England, who came to America in 1630 and settled
at Windsor, Connecticut. It was like a Wolcott to
push on to the frontier—and there was little dirt to
cover the corn in Sandisfield. Horace, a son of
Horace, was born in the Marietta home by the Ohio
in 1799. He was thus perhaps even more of a pioneer, though less of a traveler, than Rebecca
Winchell who in her babyhood had the pleasure of
taking the seven hundred-mile ride in her mother's
arms. At any rate he grew up knowing western life
under its most primitive conditions. Going as a
surveyor into the wilderness of Franklin, a county

adjoining Licking on the west, young Wolcott continued as far eastward as Granville in the year 1822 or 1823. He could not have felt like an entire stranger there, as his father had visited the settlement as early as 1811 and must have told the boy about old Massachusetts friends whom he found in the new Granville.

Horace Wolcott, now about twenty-four years old, met Rebecca Winchell and presently decided that Granville was the place where he wanted to make his home; and there his home was, for the rest of his life. He operated the Clear Run gristmill for some twenty years when he sold it to Norton Case; but he was primarily and essentially a farmer; the farm that he owned and on which he lived was a part of the original Winchell tract of 1805. It was the first farm on the right-hand side coming east-ward out of Granville. Only fifty or sixty acres it yet offered as varied a topography as any farm that could have been found in Licking County or, probably, in the State. It included: the top and eastern and southern slopes of the relatively high hill which limits the town on the east; a considerable reach of low pasture-land through which Clear Run took its way; a broad level terrace or upper bottom; and the "bottom" proper which extended down to the creek. The steepest part of the hill had been left in woods made up chiefly of maples, beeches, elms, walnuts and butternuts. A rudely graded contour-road through this bit of woods gave the farm teams access to the cultivated fields "round the hill." Thus the lay of the land was such that much the larger part of the farm being 'round the hill was quite out of sight from the house. The natural fertility of the terrace had been increased by judicious farming and manuring, while the annual overflow of the creek contributed greatly to the corn-producing powers of the rich black loam of the bottom. The farm was fenced, in part at least, with rails split from black walnut trees grown on the acres thus enclosed.

The house belonging to this farm stood perhaps fifty feet from the Newark road, close to the spot where the original log cabin had been built. There was barely room for a driveway between the house and the orchard hillside, the entire garden being on the east side of the house. Its status as one of the first-class houses of the street was established by a conventional front yard with retaining walls and a picket fence. A tamarack-tree occupied the space on one side of the short flight of stone steps leading up to the front door while a gnarled old smoke-tree stood on the other side. A snowball bush was a further ornament of this yard, with peonies and one or two rose-bushes as the favored flowers. My sister Anna reminds me that "grass would not grow under that tamarack; the ground was covered with periwinkle *(vinca minor)*; 'myrtle' we called it." A retaining wall separated this yard from the garden, and below the wall, in the garden, stood a mighty apple-tree. The bank and ground under the tree were carpeted with violets. Anna thinks "they were the common *viola cucullata,* though they were unusually large—as large as the *pedata.*" I could believe that a *cucullata* might be trying to turn itself into a *pedata* in that garden. We children had no proper respect for those violets; they never ranked, in our opinion, with the really wild flowers, nor did they receive any cultivation; they just grew there, like the myrtle under the tamarack. It was, consequently, one of our destructive amusements to hook two violets together and then pull on the stems to see who could get the head of the other's flower. Happily the violets were so abundant that we made no impression on the crop of any year.

Our father, Charles Coleman Hayes, born in Franklin County and so a son of Ohio pioneers, was a tanner and operated the tannery which had been established by Spencer Wright in 1817 on the banks of Clear Run. Thus we were not, strictly speaking, farm children, although our place included several acres with a garden and fruit-trees. However, this merely meant that the little Hayes children enjoyed acquaintance with the mysteries of tanning as a kind of additional by-pleasure. There, immediately at hand, was grand-father's farm which served every purpose quite as if it were our own. I always felt myself to be more or less of a trespasser in the fields and woods that belonged to the Wrights or Mr. Aylsworth or Norton Case; though no one ever told me to keep out and the suggestive barbed-wire fence was unknown. But grandfather's lands were mine to roam, to know intimately, and to regard at last as true Elysian Fields.

Grandfather's house was a two-storied white-painted wooden structure, drawn out, like all such houses of the time, through porch, buttery, kitchens, and ending in an immense woodhouse where many cords of wood were stored to be sawed as needed. The most characteristic part of the house was the "back kitchen" which in the original plan of the building had been the only kitchen. It represented the colonial idea of desirable cooking arrangements: a large fireplace with a wide hearth and beside it a cavernous brick oven. This oven, like the fire-place, fell into disuse about 1856; but I have heard mother describe the bakings— Saturday bakings—that were the order of the day in her girlhood. It seems that when that oven was once heated you had to make the most and best of it, filling it out with numbers of loaves of bread— different kinds of bread—rows of pies, cakes and whatever else was suitable for oven-cooking. At this time a wide open porch separated the kitchen and its adjoining wood-house from the rest of the house. On winter mornings the mother had to go out of doors, practically, to reach the scene of breakfast preparations; and she must have passed many times during the day through that arctic porch. In the summer, however, the great porch was a pleasant place; the table was set there for meals and there the women did their spinning; while the "butt'ry," claiming one corner of the porch, was the scene of grandmother's cheese-making operations.

One of the chief assets of this farm was the deep-seated never-failing spring at the foot of the hill and near the road—also not far from the kitchen door. It must have found quick appreciation in the eyes of Silas Winchell and his wife when the Winchell acres were selected and bought in 1805. That spring figures among my earliest recollections; in the 1850s it was sheltered by an ample brick spring-house around which grew various trees, mostly poplars. Stones had been placed so as to form a brim for the water which welled up from a sandy bottom and flowed leisurely out over a spread of pebbles and found exit from the spring-house on the side toward the road. In all weathers except the coldest, grandmother set her crocks of milk and cream in this shallow running water, and often the churning was done in the spring-house or in the shade just outside the door. The butter-jar kept company with the crocks of milk. It always seemed as if the richness and sweetness of that hard yellow butter was due to the running spring-water; though there may have been something in grandmother's skill—also in grandfather's cows.

On the steep hillside above the spring, reaching from the public road to the pasture-fields on the south, was the orchard. A few of the trees were of great size and must have been set out in the early years of the colony; the others were in their prime when I first knew them. Spraying was unknown in those days; indeed, it seemed not to be needed; but the trees were regularly and carefully trimmed. A small flock of merino sheep helped in the care of this orchard, for they were given the run of it whenever the grass showed signs of reaching mowing-length. Ragweeds tried to get a foothold, but either the sheep or the thrifty grass headed them off. It is a mystery now how grandfather ever secured such a variety of choice apples. Did the grafts come from the Bowling Green nursery, or the Cunningham orchard, or Phineas Ford's place on Ramp Creek? There were Red Vandevers, Gate-apples, Russets, Rambos, Pippins, Greenings, and Bellflowers; and each kind, considered by itself, seemed the best. Just at the top of the steepest part of the hill grew two or three vigorous young trees which bore what we called Wine-apples. These apples were of enormous size and beautifully splashed with vivid red; the texture and flavor quite matched the appearance of the apple. But they were an autumn apple and not "good keepers." A Wine-apple would fall, bound down the hill and across the narrow driveway and hit the house with a challenging thud. Then grandmother in a tone of resignation would say, "Well, Elly, go get it; I guess we'll have to make a pie, now." Yet as "eating-apples" they were much too fine to be used for mere pies.

The professor of horticulture, Ohio State University, has kindly furnished me with a list of nine varieties of apples that are now most extensively grown in Ohio, with a rating of their comparative merits. I do not find in the list a single variety that the Wolcott orchard contained in 1855; which must mean, so far as one orchard's evidence shows, that the old apples are gone with those old orchards. Are the new ones really superior to the old?

Although apples were the main fruit-crop there were some grapes. A mighty Catawba vine grew on one side of the house and an Isabella on the other. The modern favorites had not then been originated. Quince-trees flourished with no need of sprays, while the latest and best varieties of blackberries, strawberries, currants, and gooseberries found places in the ample garden east of the house. To this list should be added pears and cherries of which there was always an abundance.

Besides being continually after apples people came to this farm for sweet potato plants, for seed-corn and oats and seed potatoes; for rhubarb—"pieplant" it was called—for honey and asparagus. Yet the home table was never robbed nor was the family compelled to be content with inferior leavings while the best was parted with to buyers at the gate. Grandfather throve but not through hard bargaining. His reputation rested not merely on the fact that he was sure to have the best article that could be raised; he was absolutely fair in weights and measures as well as in quality—and the finest apples were quite likely to be at the bottom of the barrel. He was somewhat of a bee-specialist and diligently read his bee-keepers' journal. In 1852 Langstroth gave to the world his important invention: a hive with a movable frame; and soon after that a Langstroth beehive appeared on the orchard hillside, and a little later an Italian queen bee was housed there.

If Horace Wolcott could have been advised, sixty years ago, of the condition of the cellar in my eastern home as that cellar stands today he would undoubtedly have wondered with deep concern whether all his other grandchildren were to live in like straitened circumstances. Not one barrel of apples or bushel of potatoes—to say nothing of the lack of barrels of pork and corned beef, of vinegar and cider. Little except coal and wood and canned fruit; and what do such trifles as canned fruit and jellies and grape-juice signify for food. That a motor-truck from Boston should stop at my gate twice a week on its delivery-rounds and bring me whatever I had chosen to order would only prove against me the scandalous fact of "living from hand to mouth." In 1860 paper-bag marketing was yet to be dreamed of and devised. It would certainly have aroused grandfather's utmost disapproval if not his scorn. His own ample cellar was so stored with barrels and bins of farm-produce that one could barely pass from the stairway end of it to the other end by squeezing through narrow lanes formed by these barrels. The house was provisioned as if for a seige, though the only foe that ever invested this domestic fortress was the cold and snow of the unproductive months.

The little brick smoke-house in the back orchard supplemented the cellar. Each autumn, after the hogs were butchered, the smoke-house rafters were hung thick with hams and shoulders and bacon strips; and when a "beef critter" was killed many pieces of jerked beef were crowded in among the hams. Every morning through the late fall and the winter grandfather went with a shovelful of coals and smoke-making materials and started a fire on the ash-strewn earthen floor. That windowless chimneyless hut might have contained the shrine of *Lars familiaris,* so faithfully did the head of the house himself attend to the duty of building fragrant fires therein. But he was only providing for his family—as his father before him had done in shooting bears and wild turkeys. No Chicago packers will ever put on the market hams and bacon and dried beef with such a delicious flavor as belonged to those home-cured products that came out of the little old smoke-house.

With the exception of tea, coffee, sugar, salt, and a few spices every item of food-stuff that the family needed was raised on the farm. For root-foods there were white potatoes, sweet potatoes, turnips, carrots, beets, and parsnips. Above ground, beans, peas, cabbages, tomatoes, lettuce, pumpkins, squashes, cucumbers, watermelons and muskmelons; and to these must be added that array of fruits beginning with apples and ending with cherries. Finally the grains. Apples certainly had a rival in the Indian corn to the growing of which the soil was so admirably adapted. Besides corn there was wheat, oats, rye, and buckwheat—enough and more than enough for the family's needs.

Grandfather Wolcott undoubtedly had a special aptitude for fruit-growing and gardening; he probably did surpass his neighbors in some of the land-arts which are near sciences—grafting and pruning, for instance; yet the thrift and success that marked his farming operations were, on the whole, fairly typical of the thrift on the majority of the farms in Granville township and in the entire county, for that matter, in 1850–1860. The most important economic feature of society at that time, so far as food was concerned, was the freedom from dependence on outside markets. And this went far toward maintaining the colonial quality of life.

## CHAPTER X

# THE YEAR AROUND

Come, let us anew
Our journey pursue,
Roll round with the year.
                    —*New-Year's Hymn.*

The pioneer year, instead of dating from the first of January, really opened some six weeks later when the sap began to ascend in the sugar-maples. Those who were so fortunate as to possess a sugar-camp now brought out the wooden troughs, tapped the trees and inserted elder spiles which conducted the sap to the troughs placed at the bases of the trees. The sap was gathered and boiled in large kettles usually hung somewhere in the camp. It was cold and often wet work; but it will be, let us hope, many thousands of years yet before normal human beings cease to enjoy a wood fire out of doors. Primitive man built a fire in the open—and that explains all, or nearly all. The camp-fire, the dinner of cold mutton, bread and butter, and doughnuts, eaten sitting on a log with one's wet shoes near the hot ashes, the "sugaring-off" nights when the neighbors came over—did the round year offer any activity more welcomed than that initial piece of work: sugar-making. Our farm had no real camp, only maple-trees scattered here and there among the other trees. But we children knew how to manage so that the sweets of those few trees should not go wholly to waste. We cleaned away the leaves and earth from the large knobby roots just at the base of the tree in order to get a comparatively level surface; then with some stubby old knife borrowed from the kitchen and a gimlet from the tool-chest we dug holes about an inch in diameter and half an inch deep in these exposed level roots. The hole was presently filled with sap; indeed, the sap was in a hurry; it began running before we were ready for it. Then you had to get down on your hands and knees and drink the sap. One swallow and the tiny cup was empty. It was delightfully exciting to run from tree to tree and secure the sweet draught before the cup over-flowed. We had our favorite trees, because we discovered that the sap was much sweeter in some trees than in others. Whether we had to kneel down on dead leaves or plain bare ground, our feet and knees were sure to be damp and chilled, if not actually wet, when we went home from this sap-drinking. Small wonder that mother was usually called upon to rise in the middle of the night, bring the queer old camphor-bottle and rub some child whimpering with the "leg-ache." But the next morning we were all off again, across the fields to the trees, worried by nothing except the thought of the sap that had run to waste during the night.

The snow had now disappeared except on some spots unreached by the sunshine. Every farmer was looking anxiously at his wheat-fields and presently getting ready to plow for corn. Before anyone realized it garden-making was at hand.

Mother carefully saved seeds every summer and fall, and now she brought out her bag of seeds, each kind tied up and marked; for this was before the day of the seed catalogue and the success of the garden depended largely upon the saving of good seeds the season before. Grandfather regularly had a large hotbed and in it the sweet potato plants and early tomato plants were grown; but most seeds were, of course, planted directly in the ground. In the garden planted by father every row was straight and all the rows evenly spaced; not an onion or a beet dared step out of line during the entire season. Grandfather was much less particular; all the vegetables seemed to be having a luxuriantly jolly time on that sunny eastern slope below the house. I have since concluded that plants do not consider "toeing the mark" an essential of happiness or growth.

In the spring everything came at once. Besides being the time to make garden it was also the time to make soap. The wood-ashes had been stored in a large wooden hopper, pyramid-shaped, vertex down. Soap-grease had also been saved during the year. The useful big kettle in the back yard was now rigged up and the soap-grease put on to cook. Water, many pailsful, had to be carried and poured onto the ashes. What finally trickled out at the bottom of the leach was strong lye. The lye was added to the soap-grease and after a proper amount of boiling and stirring the soap was done. The result was a dark-brown translucent jelly— soap indeed. A barrel of it, more or less, was stored away in the cellar to be used for washing clothing and dishes and floors, though we had bars of coarse yellow soap, less strong than this home-made soap, for bathing purposes. Ivory soap and all its kind of light mild soaps were yet to be compounded. "Did you have good luck with your soap?" amounted to a fraternity password among the housewives of that period.

The Clear Run bridge where the Newark road crossed the stream was probably of wood to begin with; but in my childhood it was a solidly built, single-arched stone bridge, only broad enough for a single track with no railing to protect the foot-passenger from going over the edge. On the upper side the water ran rapidly and whirled sharply as it turned to go beneath the bridge. This spot was never a favorite place for wading: the water would knock you down; also, because the water was so swift, it was useless for fishing. But below the bridge the stream widened out into a comparatively large and calm pool through the lower and shallower parts of which, people drove to water their horses or to go down the by-road that led to the sawmill and the creek ford. This crossing-place below the bridge was reached on either side by a track much lower than the road proper. The depth of the water in the pool depended on the freaks of the spring freshets. Sometimes we found that a good deep fishing-hole had been filled up and another dug out somewhere else. The neighborhood washed its buggies in the pool and grandfather also used it for washing the sheep just before shearing-time in the spring. The sheep were driven down the ford-road and though they tried to scramble up the bank or dash back toward home, with much pushing and heading-off they were got into the water. One or two of my uncles waded in above their knees and tumbled the poor sheep about, under the delusion that they were washing them. The water was cold and not even any soft soap was used. I, who excitedly watched this operation from the bridge-edge above, was always glad when the scared and distressed creatures were allowed to go back into the "little meadow" by the barn and dry themselves in the sunshine; though even then I had my doubts about the efficacy of that scrubbing. If warm water and soft soap were needed to wash a little flannel petticoat why did not one need as much to wash a sheep's woolly coat? It now seems probable that the sheep-washing was a traditional ceremony.

Perhaps the happiest day of the late spring was the one when mother finally decided that it was warm enough for us to take off our shoes and stockings. We had grown so tired of those woolen stockings, though they were thin and old and much darned, and the little shoes were old, too, with a winter's hard wear; and now our white tender feet were set free to take their first run of the season on the soft grass that grew around the well and reached over to the newly-made garden. Excepting on Sundays when we had to "fix up" to go to Sunday-school, or on an occasional errand to town or some journey away from home, we never saw those shoes and stockings until the September frosts and chestnut-burs made us glad to put them on again. And long before that time our feet were brown and tough. Gravel, tan-bark, and even wheat-stubble we trotted lightly over with indifference, although we never lost our fear of the Osage orange thorns.

Grandfather's barn was much larger than his house and it had need to be to accommodate the hay and oats and wheat that came from the fields 'round the hill. Extra help was employed on the farm at this one time: when the grain must be quickly harvested. But as for the threshing—that was done at any time during the year as need arose. Sometimes the sheaves of wheat were unbound and strewn evenly on the threshing-floor and one man threshed out the grain with a flail. This flail consisted of two stout dressed sticks, one long and one short, tied loosely together with a buckskin string. Grasping the end of the long piece with both hands the thresher skillfully whirled the short piece above his head and brought it down so that its whole length struck the grain at once with a dull thump. Wheat-heads seemed quite unable to resist such a thumping. There was evidently a knack in threshing with a flail, even as there is in mowing hay with a scythe or in milking a cow— with opportunity for degrees of expertness.

At other times the two horses were brought in and walked around on the threshing-floor until the wheat lay on the floor underneath the straw. Grandfather certainly was an adept at divining a child's unspoken wish, for more than once he made a rude saddle with a blanket, perched me astride a horse and so I rode blissfully in this tranquil barn circus. The barn equipment included at least one piece of real machinery: a fanning-mill run by one-man power like a grindstone. After the straw had been removed from the floor and the grain gathered up it was separated from the chaff in this fanning-mill. The next thing was to go over to the grist-mill and get the wheat ground; then we were likely to have for supper hot biscuits that had been in the sheaf high under the barn rafters that morning.

The grist-mill, a few hundred yards from grandfather's barn, was the one which great-grandfather Winchell had built in 1816. It now had a carding-mill department; and here some of the wool washed in Clear Run was carded. Before her marriage mother did a great deal of spinning. She never spun afterwards except now and then for pleasure and to show her wondering little girls how it was done; nor am I able to say where her yarn was made after it was carded; but she knitted—knitted incessantly when she was not doing other work. It was necessary, for "store stockings" had hardly found their way into common use, even if they could be bought at all. So mother made all the stockings for her family; she was so expert that she could knit a medium-sized stocking in one day if it were just an ordinary day and somebody helped a bit with the usual program, which was merely one of cooking three meals, washing dishes, making beds, sweeping floors, and attending to the needs of the little ones. I doubt whether she regarded knitting as work; for I have often seen her knitting, gently rocking the baby in the cradle, and reading a book or paper at the same time. Besides stockings she knitted good warm mittens, usually of red or white yarn.

Not only our stockings but our shoes, as a rule, were home-made. The house-to-house shoemaker came every fall with his kit and bench and was established in one corner of the tannery building where he worked until all of us, old and young, were new-shod for the winter. The shoes, compared with modern machine-made products, were ill-shaped homely foot-gear; but they were made of the finest calfskin, and they served well to carry us through the slush and mud of a long winter. Our clothes were likewise home-made. Mother cut out our garments, as well as her own, and sewed them by hand; while the village tailoress, going from house to house, came when needed and made father's clothes. Our little dresses were of calico in the summer, with winter ones of linsey-woolsey, a coarse strong mixture of wool and linen. Our "every-day" undergarments were made of nankeen—a mild form of the modern cotton khaki as regarded texture and color, though much lighter in weight. In the dressing of us mother made one concession to the prevailing views of elderly ladies: she insisted, or tried to insist, on sunbonnets. How we detested those sunbonnets! I was willing to start out with one, for it continually came handy to carry eggs or stones or chips in. The younger girls often suffered the ignominy of having their bonnets tied on in secure knots under their chins. One way to meet this trouble was to push the bonnet off so that it hung down one's back like an academic hood. It was also true that much chewing would weaken a sunbonnet-string. We wore our hair cut short and hair-ribbons were happily unknown in that day. Thus we went about in the summer and autumn months, always barefooted, usually bareheaded, much browned and somewhat freckled by the sun and wind, blithe in our fitness to wade streams, climb trees, and slide down hay-mows.

For one or two days each year the men of the neighborhood dropped all other work and rounded themselves up under the direction of a road-supervisor to work on the roads; in this way meeting their road taxes. They brought horses and wagons, plows, scrapers, and shovels. The ground beside the wagon-track was plowed and then dragged on scrapers and spread over the track itself. The result often was to make possible even deeper mud than before. Encouraged by signs of iron ore and by the discovery of limestone in the beds of streams at certain places, two of the early settlers built, in 1816, a furnace near the point where Clear Run emptied into the creek. The enterprise was, on the whole, disappointing; the property passed from owner to owner, and furnace operations were at length abandoned. In 1850 all that remained to show where the old furnace had stood was a great pile of cinders. The road-makers looked upon this as a windfall; loads of the cindery material were hauled and piled into the roadway in the neighborhood of the stone bridge over Clear Run. When ground up by many passing wheels it made a black dust. However excellent the cinder may have been for the roads no child liked these repairs. The very toughest bare feet protested against the heat received and given out by that road-stuff on a midsummer day; and besides that, it could cut almost like glass.

Exactly in front of our house, in the roadway on the slope going down to the bridge there was for years a rounded stone perhaps a foot across and projecting five or six inches above the ground. It stuck there with a curious persistence, a vexation to drivers. At last, one road-working day, it was resolved to take that stone out. So the men dug and dug—it would never do to give in after once beginning. The stone proved to be much larger than they had expected. What they brought to light was a glacial boulder, two feet or more in diameter, rounded and polished, composed—I should judge now from my recollection of it—of white and pink quartzite. It would have been a thing of beauty and value in any public or private grounds or in a museum, telling its dramatic story of the Ice Age. But how could those road-makers see any value in it? "Can't go up er down that hill 'thout strikin' the plaguey stone with yer wheel." Determined to dispose of it they got log-chains and hauled it with some difficulty to the pool below the bridge and rolled it in. That bit of road-improvement took place some sixty years ago; the objectionable stone is probably in the pool today, covered with many layers of mud and *débris*, if indeed it has not been deeply buried by other road-improvements of the style demanded by automobiles.

Prior to 1850, fruits, especially berries, were carried beyond their natural season either by preserving or drying; but the preserves were undesirably rich and sweet and were regarded as an article for the company table. Apples were strung on long coarse thread and then dried in the sun or oven; afterwards they were festooned from the kitchen ceiling or hung in the attic. Apple-butter was also made in quantity for every-day use. But

sometime about 1860 fruit-canning was introduced. The jars were earthen, fitted with tin cov-
ers; after the hot cooked fruit had been put into
the jar and the cover adjusted melted sealing-wax
was poured into a groove in the jar around the
edge of the cover. It was a troublesome and more
or less uncertain method of keeping fruit, but
housekeepers were glad to avail themselves of it as
being at least easier than preserving, and the fruit,
when it "kept," was better than the dried article.
And nobody complained, because nobody imagined
the glass jar of today with its rubber-band and
screw-top.

Tallow was one of the very important by-products
in the slaughtered beef-animal, because our main
dependence for artificial light was the tallow candle. These candles were of two kinds: mold and
dip. The candle-mold consisted of a set of six or
twelve molds of the length and diameter of the
desired candle. They were evenly spaced and
rigidly welded together, opening into a common
pan-like top while the other ends tapered to small
open tips. Wicks of cotton were passed over small
sticks lying across the face of the pan, then passed
through the molds and carried out of the small
end-openings and tied in knots to keep them taut.
The melted tallow was then poured into the molds
and they were set aside to cool and harden. The
skill in this kind of candle-making was called for
when the candles were lifted from the molds by
means of the cross-sticks. All on one stick had to
come out at once; unless great care were used a
candle or two was sure to crack and be wrecked.
For the dip candle wicks of proper length were

strung on a long slender stick and the whole stick-full dipped into a kettle of melted tallow. It was hung on one side to cool and later dipped again to get another coating of tallow; having a set of these sticks the candle-maker dipped each one in turn. This process was kept up until the candles had grown to sufficient size when they were slipped off the sticks and stored away. The molded candles were better-looking because more symmetrical, but the dip candles had no excuse for cracking or breaking.

Butchering hogs, late in the autumn, was one of the heavy tasks in the year's work—heavy for men and women alike. The hogs had to be killed and scalded and scraped, dressed and cut up; then the women took hold. Besides the main portions: hams, shoulders, pork and bacon—accounted for to the smoke-house or the pork-barrel in the cellar—there was sausage-meat to be ground and lard to be tried out and last of all, headcheese and souse to be made. For days the place was one of pork, yet everybody lived patiently through the toil and grease, knowing that the year's store of food was receiving large and valuable additions.

The raising of animals for beef and pork and mutton was a matter of so much importance to those early home-fed families that no one can be surprised by the fact that poultry-raising was made an incidental and trifling feature in the program of the farm-year. Nobody thought that a hen needed any special attention—except when she was found in the garden. On the farm of this narrative the fowls got their good living by picking up grain where the cattle and hogs were fed; they roosted on a variety of perches and nested where they pleased: in the haymow, under mangers, in the fanning-mill, in various dusty nooks in the carriage-house, and in brush-heaps. Consequently, eggs were not collected, they were "hunted." Hunting the eggs was one of the happy chores that I undertook for grandmother. I used to start out with a little old basket, only half hearing grandmother's injunction, "Don't get up where you can't get down." Sometimes a new nest was found and an extra haul of eggs secured; then I returned to the house elated and demanded that she "guess now!" for her guessing was the climax. Tactful kindly grandmother; how she invariably began with some ridiculously low number, in order, I think, that I might not be disappointed. Occasionally a "setting-hen" was found, a very cross hen in no mood to be poked off by a little girl after all that trouble to hide her nest. The announcement of this discovery was followed by a consultation; what should we do about it. "W'y," grandmother would say, looking judicially at me over the top of her spectacles, "I guess she might as well go on setting, and we will see how many chickens she brings off; a stolen nest is generally the luckiest." In this manner was poultry-raising carried on, yet there never seemed to be any lack of eggs or chickens.

The "egg-money," like the "butter-money," following a folk-custom as strong as law, belonged to the farmer's wife. Those happy-go-lucky hens must have sent many a dollar to foreign missions by grandmother's hand.

## CHAPTER XI

# THE COUNTY FAIR

"Bring out your premium stock!"
—*Ring Marshal.*

Our largest festival, one comprising the whole countryside, was the annual fair conducted by the Licking County Agricultural Society. Without sentiment or ceremonies it was, nevertheless, a characteristic institution which would need to be reckoned with in any comparative study of harvest festivals in various lands and times.

Isaac Stadden had great luck hunting in the autumn of 1800; for, besides finding that company of five men around their camp-fire in Ramp Creek Valley, he also discovered the remarkable prehistoric earth-structure later known as the Old Fort. "A circular earthwork with high banks and a deep ditch inside was a curiosity" and, as the records state, he went back the next day, accompanied by his wife, to make explorations. They found the embankment to be about a mile in circumference and varying from five to fifteen feet in height, the circle being broken only by an imposing entrance on the east, on either side of which the ditch was deepest and the wall highest. Stadden or some other hunter must have early found another remarkable though less artificial "curiosity" in this wilderness. One writer of the county history says:

> Between the Raccoon and South Fork, near their junction, covering an area of a number of square miles and extending several miles west of Newark existed at the first settlement of the country a grove of the wild cherry, doubtless the growth of centuries, which for numbers, size and quality, has probably never been equalled in any section of the United States. They were thick, tall and straight, of wide-spreading branches, tolerably clear of knots, and generally sound, except those that gave indications of great age. But few of them were chopped up to 1825. Many of them stood on the works of the mound-builders. The concentric circles of many of these showed them to be centuries old.

In 1860 the cherry-trees were gone and the usual variety of other forest trees had taken their place; but the grove had already given a name to the district in which it once flourished, and "Cherry Valley" will always and properly remind its English-speaking dwellers of the kind of trees that were growing there in 1800[*].

Cherry Valley is not, however, a valley in the ordinary meaning of the term but rather a low

---

[*]These cherry-trees were undoubtedly *Prunus serotina.* "It is one of the most valuable trees of the American forests, sometimes attaining the height of 80–100 ft., with straight columnar scaly-barked trunk 3–5 ft. in thickness . . . One of the chief elements of many tracts of forests of the Appalachian regions."—Hough: Handbook of Trees of the Northern States and Canada.

bottom-land between two streams about to unite. Closely related to the Centerville plain both geographically and topographically, it was, like Centerville, a favorite district with the moundbuilders; for the Old Fort was located in this Valley and associated with it were various other more or less elaborate earthworks.

The Agricultural Society had secured this Old Fort for fair-ground purposes. It was like holding a bazaar at Stonehenge. Of the hundreds of people who gathered in those grounds each year probably only a few, if any, were interested in the fact that the great circular embankment with its inside moat and stately entrance was the work of a vanished race. It was a "curiosity"—which is quite different from saying that they were curious about its history and purpose. "Old Fort" was their nearest approach to a hypothesis, and they let it go at that. The embankment was wide at its base: thirty-five to fifty-five feet, the archaeologists now say; its slopes, long since settled down to an angle of repose, were shaded by magnificent oaks; the great trees also grew on the crest of the embankment and in the waterless moat which closely corresponded in dimensions with the raised earthwork; and besides these trees many others stood here and there, singly or in clumps, throughout the enclosed space which was itself large enough for a farm. This distribution of trees, together with the extraordinary embankment, gave a distinctive quality to the place. I was old enough to feel its dignity though not old enough to analyze the feeling; and as I had never been to any other fair I was disposed to conclude that all fairs were held on such grounds.

Grandfather's family and ours usually combined for the ride to the fair; and since the two-horse wagon would hold so many and so much it was brought out and swept clean and boards were laid across the wagon-bed and covered with horse-blankets. Under these seats the dinner-baskets and the bags of feed for the horses were stowed away; also, carefully packed, whatever small articles were to be exhibited. Then, with everything ready and the horses rather restive, we got aboard; the elder folks sedately, we children breathlessly by way of the hubs—anything to be safe in that wagon and sure of going. We joined the procession; it was indeed a procession. As far as one could see, westward toward town or eastward down Centerville, two-horse wagons, lumber wagons, buggies, sulkies, carriages, made an almost continuous line. As we went on the few gaps were soon filled because our neighbors were coming out of their big gates in their two-horse wagons. Centerville Street was familiar but it was a more or less new world to me when we turned off east of the school-house to the Cherry Valley road. Two features of that drive are unclouded pictures in my memory at this day. One was a piece of beech-woods that we passed; how many acres I cannot guess. The great clean trees stood thick, crowding one another and they were all beeches; apparently not another tree grew there. I heard nobody comment on this and nobody seemed to think it remarkable that such a piece of woods should exist. Had other trees as saplings been removed or had fit beech-saplings exterminated the others? Besides seeing those beeches the other delightful experience was the fording of Raccoon Creek. The road crossed a sunny piece of bottom-land and on the other side of the creek wound steeply up a heavily-timbered bluff. How pleasant were those few minutes when we stopped in midstream and the driver went out on the wagon-tongue and unchecked the horses so that they could drink. The water rippled around our wagon-wheels, coming nearly up to the hubs. Great straight trees stood along the bluff face and on top of it, while smaller ones heavy with grape-vines leaned over the water; the damp cool ground was rich in ferns and autumn flowers. Even the promised splendors of the fair were forgotten by me in that bewitching wild spot. But the horses had drunk and other teams were pushing for place in the water. "Hey! When you fellows goin' on?" was the good-natured suggestion received by our driver from those following us. We went on—one small person in the wagon happily reflecting that we must come home that way and the fording-place could be seen again.

In the wide space outside the entrance to the fair-ground the confusion and jam was worse than anywhere else, but we somehow got tickets and our team was skillfully guided through the gate to a breathing-spot of quiet where the horses could be unhitched. How very distracting to have to see so much in one short day! We made the rounds of the stock exhibit where many pieces of scantling had been freshly and wantonly jabbed into those ancient artificial slopes to build pens for sheep and hogs, horses and cattle. We went up and down through the "fine arts" building, the poultry-houses, the horticultural hall. Ducks and calves and squashes and cut flowers, embroidery and jellies and ears of corn—the prides of many homesteads—were here displayed, each owner intent on winning a blue ribbon. I had believed that my own dear ducks were the finest ever; and now I saw that they were not. And "Billy," our white-faced young horse Billy; could there be any better horse in the countryside? I was made to realize that there could be, though, if my memory does not fail me on this point, Billy did come home one year wearing a red ribbon. I recall one mammoth pumpkin which was certainly larger than any I had ever seen in grandfather's fields. How had anybody ever got a pumpkin to grow so big? It was an early lesson read to me at that Fair, a hard and wholesome one the full meaning of which I did not grasp until long afterwards: Try as you will, somebody else is probably going to get the blue ribbons. Life's satisfactions and compensations must be sought in other forms than laurels.

The relative, whoever he might be, whose coat-skirts I must hold onto or get lost, often wanted to stop and stand and stand at the ring-railing to watch the trotting. In itself trotting was well enough if people wouldn't crowd so against a little girl; but watching it was, in my judgment, a clear waste of time as long as there was one coop of turkeys yet unvisited.

In 1850–1860 whatever you ate in the middle of the day—no matter what the circumstances—was dinner. Nobody would have understood such a proposal as Tweedledum's, "Let's fight till six, and then have dinner." Luncheons were unknown—at the fair as at the school-house and the sugar camp. Twelve o'clock was the hour to meet at the wagon and get out the dinner-baskets. But before that time we had found uncle Charles's folks, at least some of them, and perhaps they are bringing their baskets over to our wagon. Uncle Charles Wallace lived on the Pike east of Jacksontown. His wife was Orlena Winchell, a daughter of Silas Winchell. To see uncle Charles and aunt Orlena and the troop of mother's Wallace cousins was one of the happiest features of the day. Indeed, the social side of the fair was hardly less important than the agricultural and industrial part of it. Kinsfolk and friends got together on the ground and visited while they ate. Uncle was an exhibitor; he always brought something of marked merit from that farm of his out in the black-loamed Reservoir country. When I recall his many plates of handsome apples on the tables in the horticultural hall I wonder whether I have too highly rated that hillside orchard overlooking Clear Run. Probably Horace Wolcott and Charles Wallace compared notes and were brotherly rivals, each benefiting from the other's experience.

The afternoon, if it was one of the later days of the fair and the premiums had been awarded, brought quite a new excitement; the ring marshal, wearing a brilliant sash and mounted on a high-stepping tall horse, rode around the ring and in a thundering voice ordered, "Bring out your premium stock!" They brought it out. Through the ring-opening, far over on the side where the stock exhibit was housed, came the long procession:

trotting horses, work horses and colts, steers and cows and calves—each animal with a driver or leader. How many superior animals our county possessed! I was proud to think of it—and so I woke to the sense of community, the group-consciousness as opposed to the individual. Yes, those beautiful shiny cows were Licking County cows—and Licking was my county. At the same time I felt a distinct tinge of envy of that half-grown boy—not of our neighborhood—as he came along in the parade, proud yet embarrassed, managing with much effort and indifferent success his own premium stock: a sleek dancing colt. Part of the time the boy led the colt and quite as often the colt led the boy. There should have been at least a red ribbon tied to the boy's cap in token of the colt's success. Perhaps it was also clear to older folks—the wise ones—that the frisky young animal had other points of merit not taken into account by the judges in awarding the first premium; he had contributed already to the education of the lad.

But what I saw was a be-ribboned colt in a boy's hands. They would likely never give me a colt to train; I could only chop up nubbins for calves. And they never even let me drive Billy—he was "high-spirited," they said. In the middle of the nineteenth century there were limits to the concessions that even the most liberal father and grandfather could make to a girl who wanted to do everything that a boy did. Not because a boy did it—heaven forbid!—but because of the fact that to climb apple-trees and drive horses and swim in the creek were surely the most joyful activities that any one, boy or girl, could engage in.

Where now, I wonder, is that premium-winning boy, that young "Hector, tamer of horses." Does he sit on the porch of some Licking County farmhouse, recalling the victories of his youth and suspiciously eyeing his grandson's Ford at the gate; or did he abandon the farm in the belief that success dwells in sordid towns? There is a bare chance that he is a philosopher now—having learned what the colt began to teach him.

At the close of the fair-day, tired but satisfied, we came along home through the thick cloud of dust that lay on Cherry Valley and Centerville. Climbing down rather stiffly out of the wagon we were glad we did not have to ride as far as all those people who were going on through the town and out on those westward roads. The Fair was great, but one would hardly want to go every day. There were trees at home, and grandfather's sheep were to be seen all the time. And I did not despise my ducks; they were pretty good ducks, after all.

## CHAPTER XII

# AUTUMN DAYS ON THE FARM

All goes well and the goose hangs high.
                    —*Proverb of Welfare.*

One year, further back than my memory runs, grandfather had received a premium—solid silver spoons—from the Agricultural Society for the best field of wheat in the county. We used those spoons every day and grandfather kept on raising superior wheat every year; but in spite of the wheat, corn was the crop of the farm. The rich black bottom was regularly assigned to the noble sub-tropical grain. If every other crop had failed we could have lived on Indian corn for a year and that in a variety of forms. Roasting-ears came early; there were kinds that could be speeded up to come extra early. As the weeks went on we had succotash, the appetizing Indian dish of corn and beans cooked together. Later our corn-food took the form of samp. Choice ears were selected from corn which had passed the milk stage; a carpenter's plane was inverted and the ears drawn across the blade. The samp made from this coarsely-cut corn was a dish fit for Indians or kings or colonists. We had, of course, various kinds of corn-breads made from corn which was ground at the same old handy mill across the run where the wheat went. The kind that seemed to be most distinctly a bread was known as "rye-an'-Injun," a most wholesome and highly relished bread containing some rye flour combined with the Indian meal. Even mother, careful and correct as she was in her use of English, never called this bread anything but rye-an'-Injun. By any other name it would not have been so good.

The Raccoon-bottom corn, like that grown on other creek and river bottoms of the Ohio Valley, was very tall with immense golden ears—Ceres' happiest dream of a grain. One may well marvel that such a quantity of food-vegetation could spring in a single season from a few acres of soil merely fertilized by the muddy waters of an overflowing creek.

1859 is memorable in Granville history as the year of the great frost. Bushnell writes:

All day Saturday, June 4th, a strong cold wind blew. At night a calm fell upon the air. On Sunday morning, June 5th, there was a very heavy frost, seriously damaging all field crops, gardens and fruits. Some of the corn was knee high. Some farmers at once proceeded to plow up and plant anew. Others planted between the rows, designing to take their choice of the two crops as soon as a preference should be indicated. Others relied solely on the old. The result was generally in favor of replanting.

I well remember going with grandfather down to the bottom in the morning to see the ruin; though it was probably Monday morning when I first saw the great field in its devastated condition. What had been thrifty corn two days before was now black and shrivelled, so severe was the freezing. Grandfather decided to plant again, and at once set to work to plant more seed in the hills beside the frozen young stalks, first cutting off these withered stalks with sheep-shears. I do not recall, nor can I find any record, how the second planting resulted. Much must have depended on the date of the first severe frost in the following September. This frost of June 5, 1859, was unfortunately not local; it extended throughout the State and most of the wheat was destroyed. Granville township's great concern over the loss of the corn indicates that corn rather than wheat was its most important crop.

After corn-cutting the corn was left in the shock and husked by degrees. We children were quite able to walk around the hill and to the remotest corners of the farm, but it suited us to happen up to the barnyard, sharp November mornings, when the wagon was going to get the fodder and the corn which had been husked the day before. Later, when there were light falls of snow, we went on the big sled; above all things a sled-ride must not be missed. When those first trips were made the driver had to pick his way through the field on account of the pumpkins that strewed the ground; but the pumpkins gradually came in with the corn to be heaped up in the carriage-house until used.

Grandfather's granary, capable of holding many bushels of corn, was at the north end of a building called the carriage-house—a large carriage-room occupying the centre, and a calf-stable the south end. As the building stood on sloping ground it was arranged so that the hogs could come beneath it.

The floor of the granary had a large and convenient knot-hole in it near the door. Grandfather knew perfectly well of its existence though he could hardly have guessed how many extra feeds his hogs received through it. We shelled corn and dropped the grain through, just to hear them come running—pigs and half-grown chickens, hogs and hens—all mixed up together; then we looked down to see them eat. Next to feeding himself, normal man whether barbarian or civilized has ever found pleasure in feeding the creatures he has domesticated.

But mid-autumn brought one piece of harvest work far more exciting than corn-cutting and husking—the apple-picking. Ladders were brought out, barrels were brushed and sunned, and the pickers went into the trees. Many apples fell on the soft grass but the finest were carefully picked by hand. There were the sweet Vandevers in their shining deep-red coats, the rough Russets hard as stones and noted as "good keepers," the golden aristocratic Bellflowers. And the Rambos. James Whitcomb Riley, hardly less the poet of Ohio than Indiana, understood and wrote:

> When Autumn shakes the rambo-tree—
> It's a long, sweet way across the orchard!

Whatever the fragrance of other apples, none ever approached the Rambo; who could tell whether it appealed more to the sense of taste or smell. Have the years robbed it of its delectable qualities that it can now be found only in old orchards?

A team may make a way among pumpkins and piles of corn, but gathering up barrels full of apples in a hillside orchard was plainly a matter for extra skill and judgment. Yet the wagon never did tip over; all those barrels came safely by the long winding road through the pasture down to the carriage-house.

Thanksgiving Day seemed to separate autumn from winter and to put a full stop to the outdoor toil of the year. It was a holiday for the men but certainly involved rather more work than usual for the women. On the preceding day poultry had to be dressed, mince and pumpkin and apple-pies made, cake and bread baked, accompanied with a general tidying-up for the Day. When this extra array of food had been set away in the "butt'ry" on Thanksgiving eve and leisure had come to the kitchen the young men made bullets; they would be going hunting tomorrow; if a light snow fell tonight they could track rabbits; it would be a good day for squirrels, anyhow. The lead was melted in a little shallow iron dish with a long handle and then poured into the mold which resembled a pair of pincers; the mold was presently opened and the shining bullet rolled out on the hearth. One being made at a time the bullets accumulated slowly but at length there were enough or the supply of lead was used up. Then the guns were cleaned and the powder-horns—real horns—were filled. A breech-loading, cartridge-carrying gun would have been a wonder in Ohio at that time.

And thus, on Thanksgiving morning, these wood-chopping, corn-husking young fellows, through a well-meant ordinance of church and state, had an opportunity to revert to the mental condition and physical behavior of their primitive hunting forebears. To be sure they reverted at other times; for the pelt of some animal or other was a fixed decoration of the inside of the wood-house door. Boys whose Marietta grandfather had been a notable bear-hunter could at least catch or shoot muskrats and skunks and wild pigeons.[*]

One or two members of the household went to church; the spiritual average, as well as the good repute, of the family was perhaps maintained in this way. But there were others who could neither go hunting nor go to meeting; for there was the dinner to get—more devotion to the cooking-stove, in spite of all of yesterday's work. How patiently the women submitted to that form of giving thanks which expressed itself in a loaded and over-loaded table when each day's dinner was ample.

The medicine cupboard of 1860 showed little advance beyond that of 1810. We were still without recognized antiseptics, and camphor was almost the only "boughten" remedy for aches and pains. But mother-lore and mother-wit were suffering no decline and well-tested homely and home-made remedies were known to us. Though as regarded one disease—consumption—Nature's absolute remedial requirement of fresh clean air in plenty for ailing lungs seems not to have been perceived by any one sixty years ago; and with the help of closed and darkened rooms the scourge had its own way among the young people, particularly the young women who unfortunately had less life in the open air than the young men had.

---

[*]Appendix. Note B.

Every summer and fall, mother, in common with her neighbors, gathered and dried catnip, hoarhound, pennyroyal, boneset and snakeroot. Peppers raised in the garden should be added to this list, since a gargle of mild pepper tea was a standard remedy for ordinary sore-throat. These herbs hung in great bunches from the attic rafters and the kitchen ceiling; that is, all of them except the snakeroot—it scarcely had time to dry. As regularly as autumn came we children were shaken with malaria, "fever 'n' ague" it was then called. The creek and mill-pond were regarded as somehow causing this ailment, and in particular it was charged to the fogs which rose over the water and low lands. Mother had great faith in snakeroot as a remedy for ague; so a bowl of snakeroot tea usually simmered on the back of the stove during the ague season. What quantities we were made to drink of the bitter amber-colored liquid—and how we shook with chills and burnt with fever every other day until the frosts came. On the whole, however, we were hardy, healthful children, and mother seldom had to resort to her home-made medicines; and still less frequently did she call a doctor. Yet her life must have been one of unceasing care and watchfulness; she was alert as well as busy throughout the day and at night—as she sometimes half seriously declared—"slept with one eye open and one foot out of bed." One momentous incident in our family history showed mother's resourcefulness and daring. It was late in the autumn of 1862; father was in the army and mother was alone with her little children except as great need occasionally brought in a "hired girl."

An epidemic of diptheria came upon the community; and no one knew then the desperate character of that disease—though they might have guessed it from the number of homes which it desolated—hence no precautions were taken against infection; we were all ill—all except Anna who, happily, had gone to spend some weeks with relatives. The physician called regularly, but his treatment availed little. One evening on his rounds he looked at the youngest child, Willard, then four years old; he remarked that the child was dying and that he could do nothing more; then he left us. But Ruth Wolcott was not in vain the daughter of long lines of intrepid pioneers. What was any doctor's word that on it she should give up hope for her little one? She instantly directed her helper to bring a tub and fill it full of warm water—as hot as a baby's skin could bear it. I can see that tub now, placed in the middle of the living-room floor; the room was like a small hospital ward: we were all sick there together. The water ready, mother stripped the little fellow, put him into it up to his neck for some minutes, then wrapped him in a woolen blanket and returned him to his bed. He began at once to breathe more easily; the dreadful crisis was past, and in the morning the doctor was astonished to find the child not only alive but recovering.

The varied program from seed-time to harvest completed, winter was a season to rest and pull one-self together for the coming spring. There were no theatres, no moving-picture shows, no ice-cream parlors. The community sentiment in Granville was positively and uncompromisingly against dancing and card-playing. With these worldly pleasures under ban an occasional singing-school or spelling-match in the school-house became a valuable outlet for youthful spirits. The churches vied with one another in starting and conducting religious revivals. Whether wholesome or unwholesome these revival meetings certainly cooperated with the school-house gatherings in furnishing excitement in the lives of young folks naturally keen for some emotional life. One would suppose that Newark might have afforded means of amusement, not to say dissipation; but in the 1850s Newark was a distant and foreign city—a place where you went when you had to: to take the train, or to attend to law business.

We were of course without the modern machines and instruments designed to aid in work or to promote pleasure. To see the life of that day one must blot out not only the automobile and the telephone, but also the victrola, the kodak and bicycle, the type-writer and flash-light and fountain-pen. Yet who can say we lived in privation lacking these things? We had vigorous bodies and fairly active minds. The mind had encouragement in activity for it encountered the raw materials of its environment; native ingenuity was not smothered by possession of the exceptional inventor's constructions. A pile of clean corn-cobs held sources of happiness for a child that the owner of expensive mechanical toys cannot know. Corn-cobs are adaptable; they become building timbers or live stock or garden walls as imagination's occasion requires.

We did indeed lack the wealth of pictures which the camera brings now to every home; on the other hand we were spared the comic page of the modern daily paper. It is truly to be regretted that we little folks were ignorant of the poems and biographies which "every child should know"; but we were happily unacquainted with to-day's cheap magazines as well as the cheap favorites of to-day's fiction library.

## CHAPTER XIII

# A CHILD OF THE
# OHIO EIGHTEEN-FIFTIES

Ho, my little wild heart!
Come up here to me out o' the dark,
Or let me come to you!
—JAMES WHITCOMB RILEY.

It does not need to be pointed out that all farm operations, from garden-making to corn-husking, were full of interest to the children of this story. We looked on eagerly even if we could not help, and we learned how to do things by being around when things were done. The properties of matter, the behavior of plants and animals, the effects of weather, were studied in this undesigned laboratory and we never realized that we were studying and learning. The life of the child in the modern village or town is poor indeed compared to one on an Ohio farm in the 1850s. But parallel with the series of activities which everybody recognized as work we ran another line which we rejoiced in as all our own. It began in the spring when the frost, if not completely out of the ground, had come out enough so that sassafras roots could be dug. Sassafras grew most abundantly in the corners of the rail fence that separated the fields from the woods over toward Alligator Hill. Deacon Wright's lane would be very muddy; a confused and discouraged runlet from a small spring tried to find a way for itself in that lane; hence the mud. We "mired" sometimes, and sometimes traveled like chipmunks along the fence; but we always reached the sassafras thickets, and whatever the labor necessary we dug up plenty of the fragrant, aromatic roots. Then, since the only proper way to make sassafras tea is to use maple sap, we had to beg somebody to come with an auger and tap one tree on the hillside and rig it up with spile and pail so that we could get enough sap by the usual method. This tea needed no sweetening and maybe it drowned the memories of the snakeroot tea of the preceding autumn.

Presently the wild flowers began to come. I knew just where each kind would be found and led my little band of followers to the preferred homes of the different ones. The best place of all was the wooded bank that separated the terrace, or upper bottom, from the real bottom. This bank was much too steep for the plow and as it was bordered both above and below by cultivated fields the stock had never ranged there; nor was the timber yet needed. When we children threaded its green tangles it must have been in essentially the same condition in which little Indian children of two hundred years before had known it in their hunts for wild grapes and butternuts. Somewhere on this bluff we found practically all the kinds of wild flowers that we admitted to our lists: wake-robins, blood-root, windflowers, liverwort, Jacks-in-the-pulpit, yellow violets, white violets, blue violets, spring-beauties, Dutchman's breeches, squirrel-corn, May-apples, and along with them the dog-wood, wild-cherry and papaw blossoms.

We regularly brought some flowers home—especially the spring-beauties which grew abundantly in various places; but we never picked all that we could find. If any of these various kinds of lovely spring flowers are now exterminated in Centerville the little Hayes children didn't do it! Looking back through a vista of sixty years I see those children as fairly good disciples of America's greatest Nature-teacher who

> "Loved the wood-rose,
> and left it on its stalk;"

though none of them heard the name of Thoreau or read a line of his writings until long afterward.

The wild flowers would wilt so if you picked them. We learned from experience that those yellow violets, for instance, were far more beautiful in the shade of the biggest sycamore-tree leaning over the creek than we could make them look in a dish in the house. The Dutchman's breeches were clannish and exclusive, preempting for their own use, if they could get it, a spot of several square yards of rich earth damp with the damp of lowland woods; and their generic brethren, the squirrel-corns, followed their example. The Dutchman's breeches and squirrel-corns, above all others, resented being carried through the sunshine to a house; they were much too delicate and dependent on their own home in the woods. The curious blossoms of the first May-apples were searched for in the May-apple patches, they also insisted on room just for themselves. Blossoms or no blossoms, the broad leaves were our parasols for half an hour. Later in the season we went back to these May-apple colonies and gathered some of the fruit; anything that looked so good ought to be good to eat, but the May-apple is a disappointment; one or two tastes were enough.

In June the thickets of elder in the lane were covered with cymes of cream-white flowers. We gathered these blossoms to stick into mother's beautiful dark waving hair—knowing somehow that it was the fittest flower for such a special use; and besides that, mother had happened to tell us that she wore elder-blossoms in her hair on the day of her graduation from the Seminary. Mother had graduated; we had vague notions as to the meaning of that, but anyhow she had finished school; and here we were just beginning to go. Every season mother wore the commemorative flowers, and little by little she told us about her school.

With the wild flowers came the birds. Robins first and friendliest of all; eaves swallows building mud nests high under the eaves of the south side of the barn; red-headed woodpeckers and "yellowhammers" (flickers) in our best-known woods; wild doves down toward the creek and wild ducks on the mill-pond; many blackbirds going in companies; bob-whites in the oats-field and the corn-field—how they scuttled away, those jolly bob-whites, whenever we tried to get good "near looks" at them. Meadow-larks, redbirds and pewees reported themselves to us through song or color; rain-crows were our surest sign of immediate wet weather; hoot-owls and screech-owls sent their lonesome notes to us out of the dark. We should have missed the birds had they failed to come to us, yet we were not on intimate terms with them as with the flowers and trees.

The blooming of the earliest flowers and the plowing for corn meant that the fishing-season had also come. I could not have been more than five years old when mother responded to my urgings and bent the first pin into hook-shape, tied a coarse cotton-thread to it, gave me one of her carefully-saved corks and thus outfitted me to go fishing. In time I had a real barbed hook; it was almost equal to owning a lead-pencil. Besides Clear Run, grand-father's low pasture-field was traversed by that long head-race which conducted water from the run to the sawmill near the creek. The race had some advantages over the run: its waters moved with less current; the deeper places were the haunts of catfish, those strong thorny catfish; the grassy banks were free from trees and bushes so you never lost your hook and line in a limb overhead. When the race-fishing became monotonous or unrewarding we scampered across the pasture to the more exciting run. It had quiet little pools, and tidy sand-bars warm to our feet, and some steepish grades where the water danced and eddied among obstructing stones. Being bare-footed we waded back and forth as suited our pleasure, though we never ventured to wade the race except at one place: near the foot-log where the cows had their ford. How much, in our judgment, they added to one's supper—those few small sunfish and chubs. Mother never suggested that they were too few or too small; she loyally cooked

them for us. As years were added to the original five
my fishing-grounds were extended to include the
nearest section of the creek; but Raccoon Creek was
only Clear Run magnified. I may have caught fish
that were a bit larger; the favorite place to try for
them was below the fragments of an old dam—
one of those early dams that told of the pioneers'
struggles with the creek; but the chief advantage of
creek-fishing was the greater sense of adventure
and of belonging to the wild.

And besides all these riches of streams we had
the "Reservoir." Grandfather's nearest neighbor,
just across the road, was Norton Case. These two
men were great friends, though Norton Case must
have had in him a strain of originality or eccentric-
ity which frequently disturbed Horace Wolcott's
sense of what was practical and advisable. On
more than one occasion I heard grandfather say
that "Case was a pesky fool." Mr. Case was now
the owner of the grist-mill on Clear Run. A head of
water had been originally obtained by putting a
dam across the stream several hundred feet northwest of the mill. About the year 1856 Mr. Case
decided to make another mill-pond much larger
than the old one; so with plows and scrapers he
wrecked a good smooth field by throwing up a circular embankment. The water was turned in, and
there the neighborhood was, with a sheet of water
to be known as the Reservoir. On account of its
name it was often confused with the great
Reservoir, some miles south-ward from Newark,
which in the eighteenth century the Indians called
"Big Lake." Willows were planted at the water's
edge around at least half of the bank of the new

pond, and as they grew very rapidly the place soon became attractive and won approval—except for the ague which it was believed to promote. Mr. Case proceeded to "waste" more land, a fine field north of his miniature lake, by planting it to all kinds of native nut-trees and wild fruits. Hazelnuts and black haws were soon to be seen in abundance—the young bushes were—though we realized that we would not be picking the nuts and haws when they came; because these bushes grew in rows. Whatever grew in rows couldn't be wild, and therefore was not for us. Young chestnuts and mulberry saplings were also planted there—in rows—besides all sorts of more domestic berry-bushes. I rejoiced in Mr. Norton Case's "pesky foolishness," forbidden though that promising land might be.

This new mill-pond was directly north of the tannery acres, separated therefrom by an Osage orange hedge. I could not jump over that hedge, and to go around was most inconvenient when one wanted to begin fishing right off; but by diligent bending, if not actual cutting, of some low shoots I made a sort of a woodchuck trail where we could crawl through with minimum damage to skirts and aprons. Mr. Case stocked his pond with fish and then let everybody go fishing there; yet the place was more resorted to in winter when its watery acres were thoroughly frozen over. Young folks came from town in troops and wore out the ice with their skating. It gave to our quiet neighborhood a gaiety not known at other seasons.

The reservoir was much too deep for any bathers except those who were skilled in swim-

ming; but for us children there were compensations in the "run." On midsummer days boys from
town used to come and throw low temporary dams
of stones and sand across the run, trying first one
place and then another, and thus raising the water
high enough to make very fair swimming-holes.
We kept close at home when those stranger-boys
were meddling with our stream, our resentment of
their invasion tempered, however, by the fact that
they belonged up-town; they could not live down
here in our fields, they would have to go home to
their suppers. The boys invariably did depart at
last—and then we fell heirs to all their improve-
ments. Just at dusk, accompanied by mother or
some other older person, we would go down to one
of those holes in the pasture, where the willows
grew, or further on down to the sawmill. That by-
road was a comparatively untraveled one and at
the edge of the day we were quite sure to be undisturbed in our water-frolic. It was a piece of good
fortune to enjoy home approval and cooperation in
these twilight quasi-swims. To be sure, we would
not have "gone swimming" without such approval
though we were probably regarded as capable of it.
There is hardly room to doubt that the neighborhood, as a whole, held us in disesteem as a wild lot
of little folks; this, though we never trespassed,
and we were not noisy—we were too happily occupied with our many childish enterprises to be
noisy. But really proper little girls of 1860 staid
indoors, they wore their hair tightly braided, and
they sewed sheet-seams "over and over."

Far around the hill, beyond the end of the farm-
road and standing quite apart from the woods, was

a group of three or four trees, chief of which was a tall stately mulberry-tree. Its delicious fruit may well have won reprieve for it when its pioneer owner cleared the hillside, and no doubt it had furnished material for some of great-grandmother Winchell's pies. The grass under these trees intergrown with spicy pennyroyal was always very short because the trees stood in the big pasture where the cows and sheep had free range; thus we could easily find the ripe berries after they had fallen to the ground. Convenient for the sheep too, and it was important to get there before they had nosed the berries over. My sister Mariquita is sure that we climbed this mulberry-tree by way of a grape-vine and shook the fruit off. I do not remember this exploit, but I presume she is right and that we did get up into it by means of an enormous wild grape-vine that grew on another tree close by the mulberry. Paradoxically stated, if we had climbed fewer trees we should have run greater risk of broken bones; but much experience with trees of various kinds gave us a monkey-like safety in their branches.

The mulberry could not have been very common in the primitive forests. With their valuable fruit these trees would hardly be unnecessarily felled; and if ever abundant they ought to have been so in those mid-century years. But with the exception of this tree on the Wolcott farm I do not remember having seen one in Licking County. Nut-trees of various kinds were plentiful. For instance, there was the beech-tree at the edge of the upper bottom where the ground dropped steeply down to the race—a very matriarch of a tree, much older apparently, than those in the Cherry Valley woods. Besides being small, beechnuts are often disappointing with their three faces collapsed upon a withered interior; but we could depend upon this old tree above the race for large plump nuts in plenty. The grass there was long and each season enough nuts escaped us to afford a crop of beechnut sprouts which we pulled up and ate the following spring as a special woods delicacy.

In the little meadow which came up to the barn was a favorite butternut-tree where we gathered most of our winter supply of butternuts, and at the head of the lane leading to the barn was a black walnut tree—lone survivor when its brothers went down in the clearing. Sometimes we "hulled" the walnuts there under the tree—using a little stone and a big one. On other trips we laboriously tugged the nuts home in a basket and then did the hulling with a mallet and a block of wood. But whatever tool you used, your hands were sure to be so stained that no amount of soft soap would quite remove the yellow. Black-walnut stain had to wear off. Mother never rebuked us for these spatterings and stains on our suitable if homely clothes. To remedy such matters as best she could was in her day's work; and she somehow divined that she did well for her little ones in letting them live close to the earth; the simple relations were the wholesome ones. Dainty raiment and picking one's way was not meant for Nature's eager children. And mother made a distinction between "clean dirt" and grime; we knew much of the former and nothing of the latter.

At least once in the autumn our hard-working
father would take a quarter of a day off, hitch the
horse to the little lumber-wagon and give us a ride
to some more distant walnut-tree, the owner of
which allowed us to gather all the nuts we wanted.
We wanted about three bushels and we were not
long in picking up the green balls that strewed the
ground. When the load was dumped on the grass
back of the kitchen-shed it looked almost like a job
ahead to think of hulling all those walnuts; but I
liked it better than sewing carpet-rags and vastly
better than sewing a sheet-seam over and over.
The walnuts were hulled in time, although the
coats of the last ones had turned black and mushy
and were infested with disagreeable maggots. The
dried nuts were then spread on a high shelf in the
cellar above the apples which they so well supplemented when winter brought its special appreciation of every fruit and nut that had ripened on the
trees around us; we never saw any other kind.

We went in various directions for hickory-nuts
and chestnuts, although we found few of them,
compared with the black walnuts and butternuts.
Some mornings, after a hard frost, mother would
"drop everything" and go chestnutting with us.
Our hearts beat high on all those occasions when
we could get mother out on a search for wild flowers or chestnuts, and especially to slide down hill
on our home-made hickory-runnered sled. She was
young during the years here described; perhaps
her woods-roving children rescued to her, though
tardily, some of the pleasures that had been too
largely crowded out of a work-filled girlhood. The
foragings for chestnuts on those keen autumn

mornings stand out with unfading distinctness in my recollections because we had mother along with us.

The best groves of papaws flourished in company with the sassafras on the high ground near Alligator Hill. Nothing else growing out of doors was ever more trim and clean than those papaws with their straight comely trunks and branches and their luxuriant foliage. We rejoiced in these thickets at all times, but particularly in the autumn when, after a few hard frosts, many leaves were yet on the trees and others carpeting the ground and half concealing the yellow-green fruit which had already fallen. Papaws, like May-apples, certainly look good enough to eat; season after season we were unconvinced that they were not what they seemed to be; only after we had brought some of the finest-looking ones home and tried to eat them did we realize anew that they were too insipid and rich. Wild grapes seemed to like neighboring with the papaws, although they chose somewhat larger and stronger trees for their support. The best thickets of all were thus the ones close bordering the woods, where wild grapes, sassafras and papaws lived together. From the birch coppice of northern New England to the palmetto jungles of Florida I have never yet seen a lovelier fellowship of growing things than those Licking County thickets, long ago destroyed; and they were set like softening fringes on the borders of the woods.

The general name "woods," becoming singular in my mind, means that pathless unmarred piece of forest which covered the Welsh Hills as late as

1860, because the trees were so large, of so many kinds and stood so thickly on the ground. With the feeling of explorers we would get ourselves enwrapped with woods until in only one direction were there even distant glimpses of cleared land; but to lose sight of all fields would mean that we were lost; so we took care to keep a bit of a rail fence in view. The hurricanes or tornadoes that at long intervals struck the western woods left wreck behind them in the shape of great trees over-turned. After the lapse of many years when branch, trunk and root had decayed there remained an oblong heap of earth—the earth that had been torn up with the roots when the tree went over; and beside the mound was a corres-ponding depression where the tree had stood. These mounds were to be seen, several of them, in grand-father's hillside woods and many others were scattered through the Welsh Hills forest. Caleb Atwater, writing in 1838, says:

> In May, 1825, a tornado swept across Licking and Knox Counties. Its width was scarcely one mile, but where it moved it prostrated every forest tree or stripped it of its leaves and left it standing as a monument of its inexorable wrath.

By the Granville people this was known as the "Burlington Storm" because its effects were most severely felt in Burlington township which lies north-ward from Granville. The mounds around us might well have been memorial outliers of the famous storm of 1825. But we children regarded them as Indian mounds or graves; though I never could decide in my own mind whether the Indian was buried beneath the hummock or in the hollow. Plainly there were cogent reasons for either view. The sweeping winds had a habit of filling these little hollows with leaves, packing them down and heaping them up as if it were a good place to keep such sweepings in. How fragrant and clean the leaves were and how joyously we tossed them about and burrowed in their depths. A haycock in the hay-field, now, must not be strewn about; nor may sheaves of wheat be moved—no matter how good a tent you think you could make by just taking out the inside sheaves of a shock. But no farm rules reached a leaf-filled hollow; that was our domain.

The woods probably made more impression on us because they were open and free from undergrowth; in fact, there were hardly enough saplings to maintain the continuity of the forest even if the white man had not resolved to destroy it. We were on the under side of a leafy cover and could go about unhindered and look up into the branches of these tall trees which, both in the aggregate and individually, had charm for us. We enjoyed as such the black walnuts, beeches, oaks, ash, hickories, chest-nuts, and maples. I supposed all woods were like these around my home. Intimate friendship with them prepared me to later understand and defend Audubon's exclamation: "The beautiful, the darling forests of Ohio, Pennsylvania, and Kentucky!"

Morris Schaff, at home in these same Licking County woods, writes in his Etna and Kirkersville:

Save now and then a thicket of leafy young oaks and beeches, the woods were open and free. The views off through them over the carpet of dead leaves, lit up here and there with a splash of sunshine, and now and then some bush in bloom; the grand uplifting trees, silent, and yet every one speaking; the fallen trees lying mute, some this way and some that, the moss weaving their last shroud; the wind traveling through the high tops, and now and then breaking into a sigh; the squirrels, some frisking, some sitting up on limbs with their tails proudly arched over their backs and barking huskily in complaining tones; the birds, some like the woodpeckers, chattering at their labor, and now and then a sudden flash of living color as a jay bird came by, now and then a faint trill, the falling nuts, and the evoking silence as the leaves came down—all these were given to me to enjoy again and again in the primeval woods of Ohio. I wish that there was some way that a just idea could be transferred to this page of the splendor of those woods, when on every hand there rose those stately oaks, ash, sycamores, and black walnuts, all lifting their heads like kings far up into the sky to greet sun and moon and stars.[*]

In 1805 settlers knew these forests as something to be cleared out of the way with all possible despatch. The next generation regarded what remained—and much remained—from the lumberman's point of view: how many feet of lumber would a given lot of trees saw; how many cords of fire-wood would it cut.

---

*Appendix. Note A.

Likewise, these men knew birds either as game-birds to be shot, or as supposedly injurious to crops in fields and gardens, and hence to be shot. It was one of the pathetic features of the pioneer's life that his struggle with his environment closed his eyes to most of its beauty. Happily for the world and all coming time, the Ohio Valley early lured to it a few men like the Michaux, father and son, and Audubon, who refused to "settle." They were free and they had seeing eyes; they reported on that wealth of wild life, whether bird or animal, tree or flower, that they found in the valley of "la belle riviere," the O-hee-yuh of the Indians.

It must in justice be said, however, that the formal yards of the Wild Turkey period were not destitute of trees. Here and there one was spared as being somehow useful or ornamental; and now and then one was set out. Bushnell records that in 1842 the Town Council of Granville passed an ordinance which permitted each lot-owner to take in a certain number of feet and required him in turn to make a walk of specified width "and to set out rows of trees in line, twelve inches inside the outer line of the walk, with suitable protection." Maples, especially hard maples, must have been the favorites in this planting of 1842, for fifteen years later the sidewalks on most of the streets were maple-shaded. Shade for the country roads depended on the action of individuals; there was no community cooperation. I am glad to remember one frosty autumn morning when it was my part to hold up straight the maple saplings which father was setting out on the bank above the road in front of our house. Those young trees were well and truly planted—father never did anything "by halves"—they lived and throve and in 1917 there were two which neither storms nor axe had laid low; for sixty years they have been speaking of that regard for the street and the home.

The autumn of 1858 is memorable. Donati's splendid comet, easily premier among the nineteenth century comets, hung night after night in the sky over the old grist-mill. In the late twilight we used to gather outside the kitchen-shed to look at it. The rather awe-struck tones of my elders were not calculated to lessen my fear of the long shining object; the moon never looked like that, neither did any star. What was it? I was now afraid out of doors in the dark and even more afraid to go indoors and go to bed in a dark room. The comet was of the class "scary" things and filled me with fresh fear of all those dangerous and mysterious creatures which usually lurk under the beds of imaginative little girls and boys who are only seven years old. After a while the comet went away—nobody seemed to know just where it did go; but we saw it no more above the mill. Later there were persons who were quite certain it had come as a messenger of evil: a sign of the Civil War that so soon broke upon our peace.

Mother must have known the elements of systematic botany; for she taught us the parts of a flower and compared flowers to show us how they might be alike and yet be different. Thus we learned that the good potato and the bad "jimsonweed" belonged to the same family; and, what was of less consequence, we even learned their botanical names along with those of various other plants.

The sonorous Latin names seemed to have the property of permanently embedding themselves in a child's memory; it suggests a botanical beginning for the study of Latin.

But mother told me nothing about the comet; and she could not have known the sky, or we should have gained familiarity with some of the stars. Yet how could she know. It is improbable that there was any one to teach her, and in all likelihood she never saw a sky-map in her school-days. However, she did teach us the Big Dipper and the Pole-star, and besides these stars, curiously enough, a little group which we called "Job's Coffin." I certainly got the impression that the four stars arranged in diamond-shape made the coffin; the other six naked-eye stars of Job's Coffin *(Delphinus)* I never noticed at all. The fact that *Delphinus* is a late summer and early autumn constellation agrees with the probability that we would be out on warm August and September evenings, if ever, to look at the stars. What splendors we missed in the zodiacal pageant of the round year! It does not comfort me to reflect that most children missed the glories of the night-sky then—and miss them now.

But the life a child in that last decade of the pioneer era was not all one of care-free days in the fields—I speak for the children of this chapter. For once a week there was "meetin', church, and Sunday-school," as we phrased it. We were scrubbed on Saturday night, regardless of what we fancied Clear Run had done for us every day. On Sunday morning we received a polishing-off; then we were "fixed up" and were taken or sent to Sunday-school in the Methodist church. This building was the smallest of the four churches that stood at the intersection of Broadway and Main Street—a church for each corner. Before its "modernizing" in 1861 it had two ecclesiastical features which must have been regarded as desirable if not essential in the year of its building (1824) : a gallery and a high pulpit. But in 1861 this gallery was taken out; the pulpit was removed and in its place a low, wide platform and table were substituted. As thus changed the interior quite lost its churchly appearance. However, the people who gathered in that room thought it much improved, which was the main thing.

The Sunday-school which opened at nine o'clock was probably, in management and aims, not unlike modern Sunday-schools. For me the one exciting feature of the hour was the approach of the librarian with an armful of books. But, eager as I was to read, those books ministered neither to my wants nor my needs. The kind of book that I hungered for without knowing it was the Merry Adventures of Robin Hood. Howard Pyle was himself only a child at that time and the Merry Adventures were yet to be told.

A preaching-service usually followed the Sunday-school. The men sat on one side of the church, the women on the other. The circuit preachers were men of zeal and energy; both qualities were needed by men who must carry their belongings in saddle-bags and splash through mud and storm to reach their appointments. But a sermon prepared on horseback could be as tedious to small hearers as if it were originated in a theological library. I liked the off Sundays when there was no preaching; then we could go home after that Sunday-school. It was dearly bought freedom; coming down Broadway and then on to Centerville involved meeting many persons walking to church—with always the possibility of encounter with the ladies of the "Lower Sem" of whom I stood in great awe, perhaps because they were a procession and seemed to need the whole sidewalk. Once beyond the town limits and in sight of home, troubles were by no means over; for now I had to meet a long, if broken, string of carriages and buggies—Centerville people driving to church. I fancied that they looked severely at me. "Why was not this child going to church?" And there was no back road, no foot-path through the fields. I simply had to run the community gauntlet before I was safe within our own big gate. On rare occasions I went, after Sunday-school, to the Presbyterian church to be with grandmother. Her pew was on a side aisle, a wall pew at that, and only about one-third of the way up; but it was "climbing up Zion's hill" indeed to get there; my little knees quaked curiously as I went uncertainly along until I was safe by grandmother's side. Behind us, across the aisle, and in other parts of the church I located neighbors and acquaintances; but not even familiar faces were familiar here. The decorum and solemnity of the place was quite overpowering. I was distressed lest I should not behave properly, and thus make grandmother ashamed of me. The problem of behavior seemed best solved by sitting absolutely stiff and motionless. In the high and distant pulpit Mr. Little was conducting the service; he was a thick-set, round-faced man with simple manners, and his sermons were even more incomprehensible to me than were those of the circuit-rider in the little church across the street.

Not until sunset when, with our elders, we sometimes took a walk on the race-bank did we begin to see relief from the inscrutable ordering of this Sunday. If it were summer just the fact of having our shoes and stockings on seemed to mark off the day from its fellows. So far from promoting pride or self-complacency this state of being even semi-dressed up reduced me, at least, to a little lump of docile stupidity. "Taking a walk" as contrasted with our usual free going showed it. What to me were the yellow-bellied catfish that would now and then swing into sight in that race; and of what consequence were the "crawfish" over there in the wet cracks of the rock outcrop that I should want to be after them. But never mind! The Sunday sun is setting; tomorrow is Monday, just a plain day to do things in.

Once in those early times grandfather took me with him to a political meeting to hear John A. Bingham. This was an event, an unforgettable event, to be going with gran'pa at night to a meeting which was not a church meeting and which was held in the dimly-lighted dingy town hall with mostly men for an audience; I might have known that something was amiss, because the women were so few in that meeting. Judging from Bingham's speeches in the House of Representatives (1855–1864) we must have heard stirring words that night. Though I could understand more of what was said than of what the preachers preached on Sundays I do not recall a word of Bingham's speech. What impressed me and staid by me was the fact that here were matters to be talked about that concerned Ohio, and even more than just our State; and men were going to vote on these questions.

There must have been books somewhere in Granville, but in the early years here described I did not know of their existence; few were to be seen in any of the homes that I ever entered. The little store on the few shelves in my own home consisted chiefly of books that were either wholly unintelligible or utterly uninteresting. It amazes me now to recall how, in sheer mental hunger, I read them as much as I did. In all that desert there was one dear oasis: *Harper's Monthly,* founded in 1850. One of my uncles subscribed for this magazine—in 1856 it must have been, for "Little Dorrit" was then running as a serial; the first installment was published in January, 1856. I read the pictures if not the text, as well as those of Porte Crayon's "Through Virginia," and "Through North Carolina" which appeared in 1855–56. But the truly evergreen and fruitful spots in this green island of magazine literature were the articles furnished by travelers. I recall one such article in particular: "Pictures in Switzerland," published in May, 1857 and accompanied with delightful woodcuts of scenery. It was possibly an advantage to have so few pictures. None were dismissed with a casual glance to be replaced with more and more as is the case today. I studied those Switzerland woodcuts until every detail of mountain, stream and forest was unfadingly fixed in memory. This magazine was never thrown aside as a comparatively worthless back number. Every copy was carefully saved and re-read in subsequent years. When I graduated from the First Reader and passed to the delights of the Second I felt qualified to attack the text—big words and all—that belonged to the scenery pictures of those precious Harpers of 1857. In this way proceeded that part of my education which was connected with the printed and pictured word.

CHAPTER XIV

# EARLY INSTITUTIONS

To Eudemus, greeting,
    I have sent my son to bring to you the second
book of my Conics. Read it carefully and commun-
icate it to such others as are worthy of it.
                       —APOLLONIUS OF PERGA
                           *circ.* 215 B. C.

Ho, every one that thirsteth; come ye to the waters.
                                  —ISAIAH.

It is a noteworthy circumstance that a town no
larger than Granville should have become the
home of such a number of schools before the
fiftieth year of its founding. That log school-house,
built and used in the first winter, gave notice of the
fixed intentions of the pioneers; and whatever the
obstacles that from time to time operated to hinder
educational work the community overcame them
and maintained the continuity of the advantages
which it offered both to young men and young
women—advantages that certainly could not be
found in the average Ohio town of any of those
States formed out of the Northwest Territory.

In March, 1807, seven prominent members of
the colony were appointed a committee "to pitch a
Stake where to Set a Schoolhouse and Lot out

Materials to build the same." That is, sixteen months after their arrival they felt that they must have a better building for the great purpose of education. Bushnell relates the circumstances of the dismantling of the first school-house—which did not take place under the direction of the committee:

While preparations were being made for the erection of the new building, the boys, in their evening pastimes on the common, bethought them that it would be a very jolly thing to take down the old log school-house. As it would help their sires thus much, they thought it would be a meritorious frolic rather than otherwise. Though it was on the public square, and their noisy proceeding must have been observed by older people, no one interfered with them. They first took out the glass windows with great care, which had replaced the oiled paper; took the batten door from its wooden hinges, and carried them, with all that was of any value, across the street, and stored them away at Mr. Josiah Graves'. Then, beginning with the weight poles, they dismantled it down to the joists. Then, becoming weary, they went home and to bed, and slept with quiet consciences. But Judge Rose and others thought it a good opportunity to give the boys a lesson on lawlessness. So, with one side of their faces in their sleeves, it was arranged, with Esquire Winchell as Justice, Samuel Thrall, Prosecuting Attorney, and Josiah Graves as Constable, to bring up a number of them for a sham trial. They were brought together one evening, one of them being taken out of bed for the purpose, and arraigned for trial, with the solemn countenances of parents and officials all around them. The indictment was read, the boys all pleaded guilty, and they were fined twenty-five cents each and costs. Twenty-five cent pieces were very scarce at that time, and it began to look pretty serious to them. It waked up their ideas about law and order. Then all the officers, as the boys looked unutterably penitent, consented to throw in their fees; and, finally, it was agreed, if the boys would ask forgiveness, that should end the affair.

From the same historian we learn that

Early in 1811, Elias Gilman, Timothy Rose, Silas Winchell, Daniel Baker and Grove Case were made a body corporate, under the title of "Trustees of the Granville Religious and Literary Society," to have the care of Lot No. 11, given by the company for the support of ministers, and Lot No. 15, for school purposes, to improve, manage and dispose of the same, provided the express purpose and intent of the grant be answered. Subsequently a deed was given to these Trustees by the members of the Licking Company.

This "Religious and Literary Society," representing the spiritual and intellectual side of the company's activities, seems to have been the surviving element when the Licking Land Company was dissolved. The official management of school affairs was probably in the hands of this group of men for some years. About 1820 a two-storied brick school-house was built against the hill at the head of Main Street, though the upper story was not used for school purposes. Bushnell states that the first story was divided into two unequal rooms for the common schools; "the west room, where the boys were taught, being a little the larger, although diminished by the passage way to the room above." This certainly suggests that the boys and girls were taught in separate rooms. A wood-cut of this old building (Bushnell, p. 118), made either from original drawings or conjecturally sketched from description, might be guessed to be the picture of a dwelling in Old Edinburgh or colonial Boston. At the time of its erection it must have been the pride of Granville.

In 1827 a young minister of New Hampshire birth and training came to the colony as temporary pastor of the Congregational church. He remained to serve the church and the community for thirty-seven years. While Jacob Little's duties were primarily in connection with the church, he at once addressed himself, with his characteristic practical energy, to definite educational needs of his parish—and he probably looked upon the entire township as his parish. One of his first acts was the formation of classes for young ladies to whom he gave "special instruction in the higher branches." In this work he was aided by his wife a woman of education. What were those "higher branches" which were regarded as suitable and desirable for young ladies in 1827? Mr. Little, himself a recorder of fragments of Granville history, says, "For two or three years about this time, Dr. W. W. Bancroft and myself were self-made trustees to employ teachers, to find a room where we could, and keep up the ladies' school."

The school thus begun and managed seems to have continued without interruption until 1834 when Elizabeth Grant and Nancy Bridges, of Ipswich, Mass., came on to take charge; it had now attained to the dignity of an academy with a building of its own. Two years later, owing to Miss

Grant's resignation, Miss Bridges was placed at the head of the school. She is described as "a lady of wonderful executive ability," and it is said that "she at once carried the school to the front rank and sustained it there." In 1836 the institution was chartered as Granville Academy, with eleven trustees. At the same time, a different site was secured and a larger building put up. "From the more complete organization of the school with a boarding department in 1834 until 1844 it was conducted as a manual labor school, the young ladies doing most of the work in the culinary department." In 1844 it ceased to be a manual labor school, and in the following year it passed into the hands of Mr. W. D. Moore, in whose care it remained until 1854.

This Granville Academy had a boys' department until 1833. In that year a school for boys only was established; it served the purposes of a preparatory school for boys who were fitting for college, until the new high school in the common-school system of Ohio made the male academy no longer necessary.

Meanwhile, the Baptists had established in 1832 a school for young women, beginning with twenty-five scholars. It also had a boarding department, and could thus invite out-of-town pupils. Seven years later the school was bought by the Episcopalians and was known as the Episcopal Female Seminary. Under this new arrangement its first principal was Mr. Mansfield French, a son-in-law of Deacon Silas Winchell. Some years later, the school, as an Episcopalian school, was moved to another town, while the property returned to the hands of the Baptists by whom it was used for the purposes of another school which they had been building up. This school, due initially to the efforts of Mr. S. N. Burton, pastor of the Baptist church, was to be known as the Young Ladies' Institute until it became Shepardson College.

Parallel with these various efforts to secure educational opportunities for young women was the development of collegiate advantages for young men.

In 1830 the Ohio Baptist Educational Society thought so favorably of Granville as a desirable location for an institution for collegiate and theological instruction—primarily with reference to the training of young men for the ministry—that the necessary purchase of property and arrangement of buildings was made, and instruction was begun in December 1831 with thirty-seven students. One of these students was Sam White, referred to in Chapter VI.

In 1845 the name of the school was changed from Granville Literary and Theological Institution to Granville College, and in 1856 it was again changed, becoming Denison University.

It is not intended here to give even a sketch of the history of this institution or to speak of the rather long line of able and faithful men who have devoted themselves to its interests either as presidents or professors. Because the story of its founding and development is kept in memory primarily by the denomination which has been a cherishing mother to the school; and its history is a chapter in the larger history of Ohio's educational institutions. It is enough to remind the reader that Ohio is a State of many colleges, and Granville is favorably known in academic circles everywhere as the home of Denison University—one of Ohio's very best.

Shepardson College, as an integral part of the University, is not subject to those uncertainties of fortune which beset detached schools; it has an assured status and future as a place for the education of young women, offering rich and various advantages—some of which are due to its happy location in a little town among the hills rather than in any city. One could wish that the passing decades had somehow dealt as kindly with that other school which brought Nancy Bridges from Ipswich and a series of teachers from Mt. Holyoke. Its formal work is ended, yet no one can truthfully affirm that its influence is anywhere near an end. Such influences are tenacious of life; they take themselves on from generation to generation. Looked at historically, the major achievement of that Granville Female Academy consisted in holding its own honorably and making good in the prelude to the era of unstinted educational and professional opportunities for women. The school was, wholly without intention on the part of its founders, one of those early nineteenth-century laboratories in which women—both as teachers and students—were tried out; as if Destiny would know whether the female creature had mental powers worth cultivating.

The Young Ladies' Institute and the Granville Female Academy—contemporaries if not rivals— were locally known as the "Upper Sem" and "Lower Sem," respectively. The home of the former was in the west end of the town near the University buildings, while the latter was located quite at the eastern extremity of Broadway. For geographic and denominational reasons as well as family ones, I knew more and saw more, in my early girlhood, of the "Lower Sem." Horace Wolcott was a steadfast friend and supporter of the school, a trustee, 1837–1864, and honorary trustee during the last five years of his life, 1870–1875. As an illustration of the kind of thing he would do for the school, he made it his business to see that the students had an abundant supply of fresh pure milk which he supplied from his farm, carrying the milk himself up to the school buildings. Perhaps he was paid for the milk; but knowing the man, it is easier to believe that he held this to be a service to be rendered without other reward than the satisfaction of putting one good article of food on the Academy table. When I was a little girl grandfather no longer carried the milk; but I knew how he did it in those years when he was young enough and strong enough: on a high shelf in the springhouse was a neck-yoke, carved to fit a man's shoulders; it was a single piece of wood with horizontal arms projecting beyond the wearer's shoulders. Pails of milk were hung by hooks from the extremities of these arms, while the two hands were thus free to carry additional pails. That neck-yoke ought to have been preserved in the Centerville museum which never existed.

Grandfather was glad to have a school where his daughters could be educated; he and grandmother must have appreciated that famous first principal; she was probably a frequent as well as an honored guest in their home, for one of their little girls was named Nancy Bridges. It was in this academy, under the administration of William D. Moore, that mother received her education. The school at that time must have borne the name, Granville Female Seminary. I always heard it referred to as the Seminary, or the "Sem"; and in a copy of Butler's Analogy—now among my treasured books—I find, in delicate script: Ruth R. Wolcott, G. F. S. 1848. Mother always spoke of Mr. Moore with the greatest esteem and gratitude. He must have been a gentleman and a scholar, as well as one who gladly taught. A Vermont man by birth and a graduate of Dartmouth college, 1837, he had intended to seek an appointment as a foreign missionary; but finding himself not strong enough for the hardships of a missionary's life he turned to teaching—happily for that Ohio academy. I here gratefully acknowledge my own indebtedness to William D. Moore because of what my mother gained in his class-room.

Of the subjects studied in the Academy in the late 40s three certainly were: logic (Whately); elementary botany; and the "analogy of religion to the constitution and course of nature" (Butler). The makers of that curriculum might have done worse! Thus, adopting the modern cavalier attitude, they might have viewed logic as an "elective"—to be studied or brushed aside, as the student pleased. Botany, in 1850, was scarcely deemed a man's job; it was the one gentle—and genteel—science suitable for a young ladies' seminary. But those same young ladies were at least better off than the up-to-date student who either goes through college with no science at all or "works off" perhaps one required science as a tiresome and despised prerequisite for graduation. As for the famous "Analogy"—twentieth-century teachers might use it to advantage in classrooms where the history of the mental development of the human race is seriously studied. Probably no teacher does so use it. One is also obliged to doubt whether colonial teachers with theological training made any connection between the work of Bishop Butler and that of Bishop Whately. A treatise so formal and formidable as the Analogy and proceeding from such a distinguished source was not to be looked upon as ground where one might go hunting for fallacies and sophistries. In spite of this assumption, and whatever the treatment of the text, that seminary study of Butler could not have been without distinct value.

One of the excitements of my early years was the exercise-walk of the Lower Sem girls who sometimes came as far as the stone bridge—an excitement only less than that occasioned when a "moving-wagon" passed by, or the itinerant tinpeddler arrived. These academic ladies walked two-by-two in decorous procession, one or more teachers heading the procession whilst others brought up the rear. Their progress was usually watched by me from the vantage-point of the broad top of our big gate. As they drew nearer I would slide to a position of safety and maintain a lookout by peeping through the wide spaces in the board fence. I recall one time when they opened the gate and continued on the private road leading to our barn, evidently expecting by this route to reach the banks of the reservoir. This seemed to me to be taking great liberties; for the front fence in those days was intended to show where the world left off and home began. However, after reaching the wagon-shed they faced about and returned as they came; for there, a bit beyond, was the Osage orange hedge, and even if they had discovered my own particular spot for crawling through, not one of them could have got her head safely past the thorns—much less her whole self; for it was the day of balloon-like crinoline; also, of an astonishing mode of coiffure known as the chignon or "waterfall." In some way the back hair was given the shape of a ball, comparable in size to the head itself; over this structure a net was drawn, thereby insuring to it a day's permanency. She who could maintain the largest waterfall had the best claim to style. With their much done-up hair to be careful about and their wide crinoline to be waded through, the seminary ladies were believed to find exercise in a slow march along dusty country roads. It seems rather a pity that they could not forsee what time would do with some of the limitations of their day as expressed in social convention and fashion as well as in school regulations; a pity that they had neither dream nor vision of their representative granddaughters—modern college women—training for places on the varsity crew, competing for the championship in tennis, running relay races and riding astride, and wearing a sports dress made of serge or khaki and cut bifurcate. On the other hand, it is just as well that no prophetic voice spoke on this subject to the good pastors and deacons—teachers of the people—in the Tallow Candle period. Whatever their motives for promoting female education they certainly had no wish to change the existing social condition of women. The man to whose initiative those early classes for young ladies were due must have known more theology than psychology, and more metaphysics than history of human society; else he would have recognized the risk involved in teaching a girl to read. There were analogies that might have guided him but no precedents.

That early esteem for education, viewed in all its aspects, clearly shows that the colonial conception of a school of collegiate grade was that of a buttress of the church. Thus those who so steadfastly and generously encouraged the Granville schools were for the church first. And they were wholly free, apparently, from any fear that either the knowledge or the mental habits acquired by their young people in these schools would ever lead to any challenge of creeds or arraignment of social conditions. That they were correct in their assumptions is sustained by the fact that far-reaching movements for the betterment of conditions in human society have, as a rule, originated and been promoted outside of the church and school, and often with the distinct opposition of these two institutions. The disappointments that rose to meet the sincere and single-hearted educational leaders appeared in quite another quarter: their children—especially their sons—did not want education. America's greatest sociologist has affirmed again and again in his writings that "the normal mind is hungry for truth."[*] Theoretically this statement seems to be defensible; but we are confronted by the practical fact that the majority of minds are indifferent to knowledge; that is, to "objective truth comprehended by the intellect." Study is irksome and any degree of devotion to knowledge interferes too seriously with devotion to pleasure and to business.

Most Granville boys in 1850–1860 entered manhood without the liberal education which was freely offered to them in their own community. On those kindly north hills overlooking the village, Homer and Plato waited as they have waited so many centuries in gardens and porches and on hilltops; Horace and Virgil sang there; Euclid and Newton taught all who would learn.[**] Sectarianism unfortunately held so large a place in the community life that many, first and last, sacrificed education to it because they were outside the Baptist communion. It was important to have a Presbyterian brand of algebra, or history bearing a Methodist hall-mark. Yet when all allowance is made for these prejudices it still remains true that mental inertia was such that the average boy did not seriously consider a college education. Young men like Tom Corwin and Sam White were rare in the early decades of the nineteenth century—as they are in any century. It is said of Corwin, the "wagon-boy of Turtle Creek," (in southwestern Ohio) that "he early had a thirst for general

---

[*]L. F. Ward: Dynamic Sociology.
[**]Appendix. Note C.

knowledge and was always engaged in studying some book or subject whether at school or not, when not engaged in other business. This continued to be his habit through early life, and he never lost more time in amusement or company than necessary courtesy required. He seldom permitted the social gatherings of the young to win him away from his studies." One is not surprised to find Corwin speaking so emphatically as he does regarding the duty of every voter to think.

It does not fall within the province of this narrative to inquire into the cause—undoubtedly a complex one—of an indifference to education that knows neither time nor place. It is necessary, however, to point out that Granville was not able to show herself exceptional. In common with all other college and university towns she offered intellectual treasures to her children, but they turned away to more alluring riches; she called to those of her own household, but they were not thirsty.

CHAPTER XV

# THE BURNT-OUT CANDLE

I feel like one
Who treads alone
Some banquet-hall deserted,
Whose lights are fled,
Whose garlands dead,
And all but he departed!
—THOMAS MOORE.

The close of the Tallow Candle period falls practically midway between those first years of Ohio's
existence as a State and the second decade of the
twentieth century. Midway as regards time; but in
prevailing social customs and beliefs 1860 was
much more closely related to 1805 than to 1918.
Applied physics: the electric car, the motor-boat,
and the automobile, wireless telegraphy, moving
pictures and the telephone, have wrought read-
justments to an old environment and these material changes are paralleled by modifications of
earlier theories concerning standards of duty and
conduct and ideals of social justice. If much less
was said in 1850 about democracy and liberty it is
also true that in some respects less needed to be
said. It was a premachinery period, cheap-land
period. Few individuals, if any, in the States of the

Northwest Territory had become very wealthy; nor had those economic conditions yet appeared which made possible the phenomenon of a class living in poverty. A social differentiation as regarded riches and poverty did not set in until after the Civil War.

As an agricultural region the major part of the community lived outside the towns and villages; and in that important roomy life everybody killed hogs and sheared sheep and cooked for harvest hands. These activities made a bond of common interest and while they lasted we breathed a pioneer and democratic atmosphere. If an errand was necessary a child was sent; and he walked, for the bicycle was not [invented]. Or, if the distance was too great and the need urgent, somebody went on horseback. As a result, proposed errands were all tested by the question of actual urgency. Men of the timber-lands, like those of the grass-lands, were compelled to supplement their own legs with the horse's stronger ones in the daily need of getting about the country. The horse was thus a motor of so much value that horse-stealing naturally ranked as the most flagrant of offenses in the robbery line of crimes.

Granville's public connection with Newark was an omnibus, a four-horse lumbering vehicle which began running in 1849. We who dwelt by Clear Run could hear this omnibus as it rounded the shoulder of the big hill; it came clattering down the road and over the stone bridge and disappeared from sight behind the next high ground, rumbling and creaking as it went. The driver—and perhaps the intelligent horses—knew the many mud-holes on that six-mile road, especially in the early spring when the frost was coming out of the ground. The worst pulls were over the two steep hills just west of the Dugway. Yet it was a pleasant journey—at least one judged it must be when Denison students, at the beginning and ending of the school terms, packed the interior of the omnibus and swarmed hilariously over the top of it, carpet-bags in hand.

Today a scientifically-built highway has made a memory of those old dirt and gravel roads; and a memory also of many a green bank and flower-grown brookside and noble tree. For the highway of the automobile is ruthless and overbearing. The final impression left with one who travels it is that the country is unimportant; the great business or pleasure is to go and get to some distant point. All obstacles must clear the way. Country delights that once greeted the foot-goer or the horse-borne traveler have given place to the joys of velocity. Yet these cylindered machines, in partnership with the telephone, have so largely ended the isolation and loneliness of the farm that they may well expect forgiveness. Only the people of the log cabin in the clearing with the ox-team and the dirt road knew how profound the loneliness could be on the settlement's borders. Farm isolation was marked enough even in 1850.

The decorum of our Presbyterian church forbade visiting in the aisles or on the steps of the "house of worship." I am sure of this church, though a like restraint undoubtedly marked the behavior of sister congregations. The members of each flock had glimpses, at least, of one another and were content to wait for the real social opportunities afforded by the quilting-party and the job at the blacksmith shop. The "early candle-light" gatherings: the midweek prayer-meeting, the spelling-school and singing-school, also offered compensations for the proprieties that marked Sabbath assemblings. Eager to go to these community meetings we trudged and stumbled along the uneven roads which were muddy in wet weather and full of frozen ruts bridged with films of ice in winter, our way uncertainly lighted by the moon; or, if it were a moonless night, by an even more uncertain lantern carried by someone who walked in front. We went, it seems to me now, just "to see folks." The deep-seated primitive desire for group companionship found satisfaction in these occasional night gatherings after the day's work was done.

As to lanterns—the candle rigged to go out-o'-doors—the first that I remember was made of perforated tin. A sheet of this tin had been rolled into a cylinder five or six inches in diameter and capped with a conical top; a little door by which a short candle was placed in a tin socket and a bail for carrying completed this simple lantern. In time it was replaced by a square lantern consisting of four pieces of glass set into a metal frame with one side hinged and opening to admit the candle. The second lantern was regarded as a great improvement: the light shone through glass instead of little holes in a piece of tin. One lantern or the other was necessary whether we had to go to the barn on after-dark duties or to the school-house for evening pleasures.

But, as a rule, we were indoors when darkness fell and the soft lights that shone through the small-paned windows were made by tallow candles. The picture of grandfather Wolcott's fireside was as familiar as that of my own home. Grandfather had his favorite brass candlestick; it was built saucer-shaped with a short tube rising from the center. Old and battered but of real brass, years of polishing had not worn through to any baser metal. Holding his paper in his left hand and this candlestick in his right grandfather read on and on until his bedtime, undisturbed by the fireside talk around him. The tallow ran down and occasionally dropped on his hand or the paper, and now and then he paused long enough to use the snuffers on his candle. The snuffers, black and made of iron, worked like a pair of scissors, but they had a boxlike arrangement mounted on the blades which caught the bit of wick when cut off. The paper was usually the New York *Tribune,* Greeley's *Tribune* established in 1841. Grandfather was probably one of its early subscribers. The writings of the great editor suited him; he believed in the far West to which young men were editorially exhorted to go. Good judgment and perhaps some sense of duty must have influenced him to "stay by the stuff"— the little Ohio farm which had so long claimed his care and rewarded his skill; otherwise he would have been off to the Missouri country which was then "out West." He contented himself with outfitting his boys one after another. I recall one morning when a team of valuable horses with a trim new moving-wagon stood at the big gate by the spring. There were some sheep; horses and sheep were headed west. Grandfather had thought of everything for the journey and for the new home beyond the Mississippi.

His pioneer heart must have stirred with longing for a share of his son's adventure; but he turned with silent resignation to his days in the familiar fields 'round the hill and his evenings with the *Tribune*.

Grandmother had her candle, too; it usually illuminated a page of a leather-bound volume of Scott's Commentaries on the Old Testament which lay open on her lap. Her chair was always flanked by an enormous work-basket which certainly had half a bushel of socks to be darned and garments to be mended. The Children of Israel disputed with this basket for attention, and often neither won; for grandmother was keenly interested in the public affairs of her owntime and would stop both reading and mending to share in the fireside discussions which her elder children started. She read the *Tribune* afternoons in the brief half-hour when she was lying down in her bedroom and supposed to be resting. Grandmother rarely smiled, and I cannot remember ever seeing her laugh; but instead of smiles and laughter there dwelt on her face a look of grave and kindly sympathy controlled by a cautious appraisement of your remarks and arguments. She was a person of few words, but what she said could be depended on both for truth and good judgment. Of the entire band that built Granville probably no other member more completely summed up in character the distinctive pioneer traits: hardihood, in-

trepidity, thrift, moral sturdiness, than did
Rebecca Winchell Wolcott. She lived to see many
changes—the changes of the first three-quarters of
the nineteenth century; but she belonged essentially to the decades of frontier simplicity and frontier risks. I cannot construct any picture of her in
the midst of twentieth-century conveniences and
appointments. I cannot, for instance, imagine her
taking a telephone receiver from its hook to ask
Mr. Merriman how much he is paying for eggs; or
stepping into a low easy car to go to church. Some
boy would be going "up town" and he is charged to
stop at Mr. Merriman's place and ask about eggs.
On Sundays she climbed with difficulty up into the
little buggy and one of her sons drove to church.
This buggy had no rubber tires—nobody's buggy
had them; the seat had no back support; such supports were an unthought-of luxury in that day—at
least it was not a feature of the cramped little two-
passenger run-a-bout that we called a buggy. As I
review the circumstances of this grandmother's
life I am quite sure that hidden away somewhere
in her cap-bands she carried a scallop-shell of
philosophic quiet.

The obtrusive quality of the highway and the
shorn condition of the hills are the features which
most impress the wayfarer who returns after a
long absence and enters Granville by Centerville
street. Various scratches—driveways—break
Nature's grading of the hillsides; yet the valley
and the bordering ranges of hills, viewed as a
whole, retain all their old-time loveliness. The
Town Spring once so prized is now neglected and
unused. It shall be for community use "as long as

water runs," said Jesse Munson in giving the
spring to the Granville land company. Such times
as were measured by the free running of the
waters of that spring have come to an end. Bits of
retaining walls throughout the town as well as
foundations of various old houses—walls and foundations built of native stone—speak eloquently of
the skilful masonry of the pioneers. But whether
in the town itself or in its outskirts the remnants
are few that testify to building activities in the
turkey and tallow candle days. Silas Winchell's
gristmill and Spencer Wright's tannery have
utterly disappeared and with them the saw-mill
near the mouth of Clear Run. The circular banks
of Norton Case's reservoir and the long sinuous
ones of the saw-mill head-race might now be easily
confused with the neighboring earthworks of the
mound-builders. As for Clear Run—Nature's own
fashioning of a little waterway—I have in an earlier chapter hinted at the fate of Clear Run.

Careful search identifies the spot where the
noble mulberry doubtless stood. It is marked by
the blackened and decayed snags of a stump barely
projecting above the ground . . . No, I am mis-
taken; there is no stump, worn by fire and
weather, on that spot. I see again the proud tree
and the mighty grape-vine in all their strength and
vigor. And across the reaches of sixty years I hear
a sweet voice singing:

> "Oft in the stilly night,
>     Ere slumber's chain has bound me,
> Fond Memory brings the light
>     Of other days around me";

the soft music has the wistfulness that one feels in Beethoven's Minuet in G. It is twilight and the sleepy play-worn children clustering around the singer's chair are the same ones who dashed along the race-bank and up through the woods in the early morning to get the mulberries.

The crowded stones in Granville's colonial "burial lot" and its neighboring cemetery bear the names of many of those early settlers. *Migratorius* might well be cut beneath each name. They were pilgrims indeed; yet they camped long enough among their chosen sheltering hills to write one of the heroic introductory chapters for the history of the first State formed from the Northwest Territory.

# APPENDIX

*Note A.* The reader will say, "Your trees loom large in memory, but how large are they in reality?" In justification, therefore, of Morris Schaff's statements as well as my own I give the following facts taken from Gray, Manual of Botany; Fuller, Practical Forestry; Hough, Handbook of the Trees of the Northeastern United States and Canada.

1. Black Walnut.—A large and handsome tree often 90 to 150 ft. high (Gray); trunk 4 to 6 ft. in diameter (Hough); if the trees had been left standing they would now be worth many times more than the land is, from which they were so ruthlessly destroyed (Fuller).

2. Shell-bark Hickory.—Large and handsome tree, 70 to 90 ft. high or more, of great economic value (Gray); this stately hickory occasionally attains the height of 120 ft. and 3 or 4 ft. in diameter of trunk (Hough).

3. White Ash.—A large and very valuable forest tree (Gray); one of the most valuable hardwood trees of the American forest and one of the stateliest representatives of its genus (Hough); reaches a height of 70 to 80 ft. (Hough).

4. White Oak.—Attaining under most favorable conditions when growing in the forest, a height of 150 ft. and trunk 4 to 5 ft. in diameter (Hough); stem 6 ft. and sometimes more in diameter (Fuller).

5. Beech.—75 to 100 ft. high (Gray); straight columnar trunk 3 or 4 ft. in thickness. One of the most distinct and beautiful trees of our American forests (Hough).

6. White-wood (Tulip-tree).—A most beautiful tree, sometimes 140 ft. high and 8 to 9 ft. in diameter in the Western States (Gray); in the valleys of the streams tributary to the Ohio River individuals have been found to attain the height of from 150 to 190 ft. with columnar trunks 8 or 10 ft. in diameter and free from branches to a height of from 80 to 100 ft. (Hough).

7. Sugar Maple.—Often reaches a height of 80 to 90 ft. with a stem 3 to 4 ft. in diameter (Fuller); the stately Sugar Maple in the forest sometimes attains the height of 100 ft. or more with trunk 3 to 5 ft. in diameter (Hough).

8. Sycamore.—Our largest tree, often 90 to 130 ft. high with a trunk 6 to 14 ft. in diameter (Gray); the stems of large specimens often becoming hollow only a shell of 3 or 4 inches remaining sound. These old hollow trunks were utilized by the early settlers in Western New York, Ohio and Indiana for grain-bins, smoke-houses and similar purposes (Fuller).

One historian of Licking County relates that a pioneer family in the South Fork bottoms lived for a year or more in a hollow sycamore-tree. When they got a better house the sheltering sycamore was ungratefully felled and "the stump kept to fatten hogs in. It was at least 10 ft. in diameter."

*Note B.* Morris Schaff's testimony ought to be added to all that has been recorded in recent ornithological literature regarding the former abundance and later absolute disappearance of the wild pigeon. In Etna and Kirkersville Schaff says:

But the game bird that overshadowed all others in its numbers, and left the greatest gap by its sudden and, I fear, complete destruction, was the wild pigeon. The fate of this strong-winged, far-ranging, and tameless bird is pathetic. They are all gone. Once they darkened the sky. Millions of them flew over Etna Township as they traveled to and from their feeding-ground to their roost in Bloody Run swamp. The pigeons set toward the roost about an hour before sundown, often lighting in the intermediate timber for a while, and then passed on in a broad stream as far as the eye could reach. After arriving at the swamp they circled round and round till dark, when they settled down, covering every limb and twig. I never went there but once, and then in company with some of the farm hands. It was late autumn, and a fleet of heavy clouds was sailing across a full moon. We entered the swamp from the north side, about opposite the big island. The party was equipped with single-barrel shot-guns and old percussion muskets, with the barrels cut off to shotgun lengths. We all went in together, but not more than a few rods, when the men began to shoot. The birds would rise in throngs, with thundering noise, but would soon come back, for there were hunters, apparently, all along the margins of the swamp, and the firing was like that of a closely engaged skirmish line. When the pigeons returned they would light all over and around us, and no aim was necessary, or possible, for that matter. We carried away two large three bushel bags full by nine o'clock, and doubtless did not get one half of what we killed. The owls and minks that infested the swamps lived on what we left. By ten o'clock the firing ceased, and the poor creatures could then find peace for the rest of the night . . . The pigeons left the swamp about daylight in vast columns several miles in length, and would fly off to their various feeding grounds, distant from one to over two hundred miles.

They fed all through the beech woods, and it was most interesting to see them feeding. If they were approaching, there would be the appearance of a blue wave four or five feet high rolling toward you, produced by the pigeons in the rear flying to the front. When startled while feeding, their sudden rise would sound like rumbling thunder. The last time they nested in Licking was about 1845 or 1846. I fix that date, for my visit to their nesting grounds in the big woods with my father is about my first remembrance. The nests were constructed of small twigs laid up loosely and very carelessly, apparently; and yet I used to see the remains of some of them when fox-hunting through these woods eleven or twelve years after they were made . . . From 1860 to 1870 the destruction of the wild pigeons went on at an astounding and deplorable rate, chiefly by netting; and in 1880 they had almost disappeared . . . Had any one standing under a broad flight in 1850 predicted that in less than fifty years not one would be left, he would have been set down as a dismal crank. But so it is and, now with the fate of the wild pigeon in view, we are compelled to believe that the doom of the wild turkey, swan, woodcock, the upland plover, the most innocent of all birds, is sealed. In the light of this slowly approaching calamity, a hunter who comes in with more than two of any of our game birds should be looked on with aversion.

It is obvious that in central Ohio, at least, the wild pigeon was the successor of the wild turkey as a game bird—making up in numbers what was lacking in size. I remember, as a very little girl, seeing my uncle, Edward Wolcott, and other young men start off pigeon-shooting. They brought back many scores of birds—needing good-sized grain-bags to carry their game in. These Granville boys no doubt went to the great roost in the swamp of which Schaff writes.

*Note C.* The first published course of study at the Granville Literary and Theological Institution is dated 1836 and reads as follows:

## FRESHMAN CLASS

| *First Term* | *Second Term* |
|---|---|
| Algebra—Bridge's. | Davies' Legendre. |
| Latin—Livy—Folsom's | Latin—Tacitus. |
| Greek—Xenophon. | Greek—Plato or Herodotus. |
| Roman Antiquities. | Grecian Antiquities. |

## SOPHOMORE CLASS

| *First Term* | *Second Term* |
|---|---|
| Applications of Algebra to Geometry. | Conic Sections and Topography |
| Plane and Spherical Trigonometry. | Latin—Horace. |
| Latin—Horace. | Greek—Euripides. |
| Greek—Homer | Natural Theology—Paley. |
| Rhetoric—Newman's. | |

## JUNIOR CLASS

| *First Term* | *Second Term* |
|---|---|
| Natural Philosophy— Olmstead | Natural Philosophy— Olmstead. |
| Latin—Cicero de Oratore. | Greek—Sophocles. |
| Logic—Whately. | Rhetoric—Whately. |
| Chemistry. | Geology and Mineralogy. |

## SENIOR CLASS

| *First Term* | *Second Term* |
|---|---|
| Astronomy. | Moral Philosophy— Wayland. |
| Intellectual Philosophy. | |
| Latin—Juvenal or Terrence. | Butler's Analogy. |
| Evidences of Christianity. | Political Economy—Say. |
| | Greek—Demosthenes. |

# AFTERWORD

## ELLEN HAYES
*Granville Author, Political Radical, and*
*Wellesley College Mathematician*

In 1920, a charming book appeared about the early days of Granville written by a daughter of Granville but one who had lived in Massachusetts most of her adult life. *Wild Turkeys and Tallow Candles*, written by Ellen Hayes, is a moving narrative and descriptive account of the early days in Granville Village and Township.

Ellen Amanda Hayes was born in Granville on September 23, 1851. She was the oldest of five daughters and two sons in her family. Her father, Charles Coleman Hayes, who later served in the civil war as an officer, earned his livelihood as a tanner. Ellen's mother, Ruth Rebecca Wolcott Hayes, was a direct descendent of the founding settlers of Granville. Ellen's grandmother, Rebecca Winchell Wolcott, was the six-month-old babe who in 1805 was carried on horseback in the arms of her mother, Ruth Rose, all the way from Granville, Massachusetts, to Granville, Ohio. One can well imagine that Grandmother Wolcott charmed and regaled her young granddaughter with stories of the early days in Granville, the fodder from which emerged *Wild Turkeys and Tallow Candles*. Grandfather Wolcott served as a Trustee of the Granville Female Academy and Ellen's mother had graduated from this early institution located on East Broadway and dedicated to the education of young women. The family home, where Ellen was born, is the red sided structure of painted brick still standing on the north side of the Newark-Granville Road just west of the Church of St. Edward the Confessor. Another Granville woman of letters, Minnie Hite Moody, later inhabited this red house, standing on the east bank of Clear Run.

Raised in a family devoted through at least two generations to education broadly construed, Ellen early on was home-schooled by her mother. Ellen acquired the skills of reading and writing and also was taught elemental topics in astronomy and botany. At the age of eight, Ellen began her more formal education at the Centerville school, located about a mile and a half east of Granville Village on the way to Newark. Today's Newark-Granville Road originally was named Centerville Street.

Long interested in teaching, upon the completion of her Granville education, Ellen taught school in the rural regions for five years. Saving earnestly from her meager salary in order to further her education at the collegiate level, Ellen entered Oberlin College in 1872; Oberlin was the first college in the United States to have a firm policy of co-education. Ellen appears to have spent three years at Oberlin in preparatory work prior to her matriculation as an official undergraduate student, which she did in 1875. Ellen graduated three years later, in 1878 with a B.A. Oberlin fostered an abiding and consuming interest in mathematics and the sciences, fields in which she was to spend her later career as a nationally acknowledged member of the Wellesley College faculty. At Oberlin, Ellen also immersed herself in history and English literature and studied Greek and Latin. This well-rounded education would assist her immensely in her later efforts as advocate and public speaker on behalf of social change and women's suffrage.

Following her graduation from Oberlin, Ellen spent one year as an instructor at Adrian College in southern Michigan. The next year, she received an appointment to Wellesley College, then in the nascent years of its existence as an undergraduate college for women, earmarked to transcend the limits of what was known in the late nineteenth century as "seminary" education for women. It is interesting to note that Wellesley, even at this early moment in its existence, was building a faculty strong in the sciences, a role Ellen was to play for her nearly forty-year stint as a prominent member of the Wellesley faculty. Wellesley itself was one of the first colleges in the country to embark on the project of developing scientific laboratories for empirical studies by its students.

Ellen joined the Mathematics Department at Wellesley, and within ten years, she was appointed professor and head of the department. In 1897, Wellesley created a new Department of Applied Mathematics and Ellen was appointed its first head. In 1904, this department was enlarged and became the Department of Astronomy and Applied Mathematics, again with Ellen as its head.

Her work in mathematics was recognized nationally when in 1891, Ellen was elected a member of the New York Mathematical Society, which later became the American Mathematical Society. Ellen was one of the first six women elected to membership in this organization. Yet one historian of science writes that Ellen's most important piece of original scientific scholarship was accomplished in astronomy. In 1887-88, Ellen was a participant in the astronomical observing sessions conducted at the Leander McCormick Observatory of the University of Virginia. During these astronomical observations, Ellen conducted research on one of the minor planets (Minor Planet 267) and she spent time calculating its orbit. In the next decade, Ellen also undertook observations of a comet, the results of which were published in the May 1904 issue of *Nature*.

A prolific writer, within a ten year period, Ellen authored several textbooks in mathematics: *Lessons in Higher Algebra* (1891; revised edition, 1894); *Elementary Trigonometry* (1896); *Algebra for High Schools and Colleges* (1897); and *Calculus with Applications: An Introduction to the Mathematical Treatment of Science* (1900).

Ellen was dramatically active in social causes. One historian writes the following about the radical tendencies of Granville's own Ellen Hayes:

> A dauntless radical all her days, in the eighties she was wearing short skirts; in the nineties she was a staunch advocate of Woman's Suffrage; in the first two decades of the twentieth century, an ardent Socialist. After her retirement, and until her death in 1930, she was actively connected with an exper-

iment in adult education for working girls.
Fearless, devoted, intransigent, fanatical, if you
like, and at all times a thorn in the flesh of the
trustees, who withheld the title of Emeritus on
her retirement, she is remembered with enthusi-
asm and affection by many of her students.

During her last years at Wellesley, Ellen found it
more difficult to get a hearing for her programs of
social reform. The Trustees, in particular, found
her positions on education and politics not easy to
live with. Along with the rights of women to vote
and to have full access to education, Ellen also
fought for the rights of the trade unions. One historical note suggests that these positions resulted
in threats on her life and her being arrested at
least once. Her political views were liberal and to
the left at a time when the Robber Barons held
sway over the collective imagination of many
Americans. Ellen regarded herself as a socialist.
Well-known in New England socialist circles as an
energetic spokesperson for these political positions, in 1912 Ellen was nominated for the position
of Secretary of State in Massachusetts on the
Socialist Party Ticket. This nomination made her
the first woman to be a candidate for a state elective office in Massachusetts. Although at this time
women had not yet received the right to vote,
Ellen received nearly fourteen thousand votes
from male registered voters, which was more votes
garnered in that election than received by any
other socialist candidate.

Long committed to the education of working
class women, in the last year of her life, Ellen
established the Vineyard Shore School, which was

located in West Park-on-the-Hudson, New York. This institution functioned as a summer school for these women.

Following her retirement from active teaching at Wellesley, Ellen turned to other genres of writing. It was in this period that her delightful Granville narrative, *Wild Turkeys and Tallow Candles*, appeared. Shortly before her death in 1930, Ellen published a historical novel titled *The Sycamore Trail* (1929).

Ellen Hayes died on October 27, 1930. Following cremation, a burial was in Maple Grove Cemetery, where her tombstone can be located today.

—ANTHONY J. LISSKA
*Denison University*
November 2004

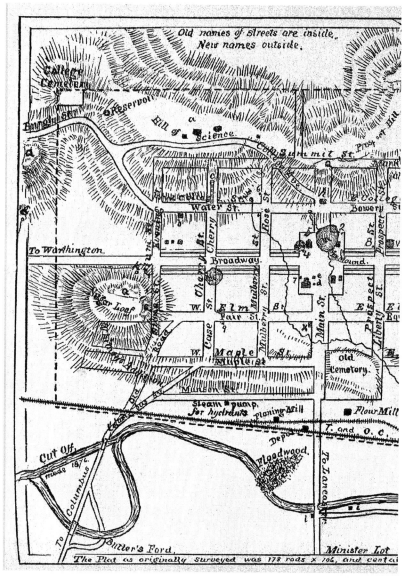

This map appeared in *The History of Granville* by Henry Bushnell, published in 1889.

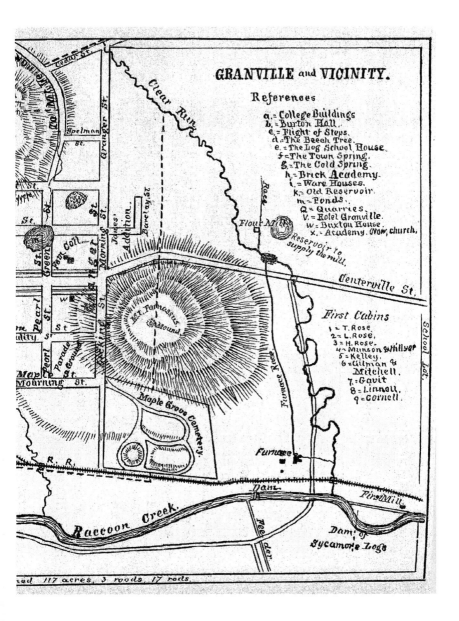

174

## THE GRANVILLE HISTORICAL SOCIETY

Charles Webster Bryant, Crayton Black, and Francis Shepardson chartered the Granville Historical Society on March 9, 1885. Charles W. Bryant with the Reverend Henry Bushnell began work on a history of the community. We are forever in Bryant's debt for genealogical records and his careful documentation of gravestones in the Old Burying Ground in 1886 shortly before his untimely death later that year. Bushnell published the historical section as *The History of Granville, Licking County, Ohio*, in 1889.

The Reverend Jacob Little, a remarkable moral force in the community wrote the first historical record, published in installments. At the Centennial of the Village in 1905, an entire issue of *The Old Northwest Genealogical Quarterly* was devoted to Granville. Ellen Hayes wrote a charming work on the changing world with the transition to artificial light and industrial progress in *Wild Turkeys and Tallow Candles*, published in 1920. The Sesquicentennial of the Village in 1955 produced a new comprehensive history, *Granville, the Story of an Ohio Village*, by William T. Utter.

A very visible and useful legacy of the sesquicentennial is the museum housed in the 1816 building that had been the Bank of the Alexandrian Society. The possessions of the Society found a home there, along with the rich archives of the society with records and images of the past two hundred years.

Governed by a Board of managers, the Society publishes a quarterly, *The Historical Times*, presents programs of local historical interest, and in 2000 conducted an oral history project to verbally document the past fifty years. It presents an award to the Historian of the Year, and an annual award to a High School student who excels in history. The Society maintains the Museum and the Old Academy Building, built as a school in 1833.